101

IRISH LIVES

101

IRISH LIVES

John Chambers

GILL AND MACMILLAN

Published in Ireland by
Gill and Macmillan Ltd
Goldenbridge
Dublin 8
with associated companies in
Auckland, Budapest, Gaborone, Harare, Hong Kong, Kampala, Kuala Lumpur, Lagos, London, Madras, Manzini,
Melbourne, Mexico City, Nairobi, New York, Singapore, Sydney, Tokyo, Windhoek
© John Chambers 1992

Editoral Consultant: Roberta Reeners
Designed and illustrated by Graham Thew
Print origination by
Seton Music Graphics Ltd, Bantry, Co. Cork
Printed by Colour Books Ltd, Dublin

A catalogue record is available for this book from the British Library.

CONTENTS

Preface

These 101 lives include actors, artists, athletes, boxers, business leaders, entertainers, explorers, novelists, nurses, pirates, poets, politicians, priests, rebels, rock stars, saints and soldiers. Some were born outside Ireland, others spent much of their lives abroad, but all are steeped in Irish life and rooted in Ireland's culture and history.

These pages will introduce you to many strange people including a pirate queen, an inventor of submarines, a blind harpist, a priest who built an airport, a revolutionary who won the world's top Peace Prizes, a general who had a boot named after him, a rock star who united the world to fight famine, a chieftain who is said to have bitten faces of dead enemies on the battlefield and a mathematician who scratched out a famous theory on a canal bridge.

Many of the people featured are from the past but the collection also includes Mary Robinson, Bono, Stephen Roche, Gay Byrne, Bob Geldof, George Best, Seamus Heaney, Shaun Davey, John Hume, Paddy Moloney, Brian Friel, Neil Jordan, Christopher Nolan, Eamonn Coghlan, Maureen Potter, Tony O'Reilly, Sean Kelly, Ronnie Delany, Barry McGuigan, Tony Ryan and Terry Wogan as well as many other living personalities.

Lives brimming with courage, excitement, terror, despair and humour make for a dazzling range of achievement. Some overcame obstacles like illness, poverty, failure in school, unemployment and rejection to make lasting contributions to society. The successes of these men and women are testaments to human determination. I hope that their achievements inspire you and that these short accounts of their lives sharpen your appetite for further research.

John Chambers
June 1992

Acknowledgments

Dave Baker, *The Irish Field*; Jackie Bennett, Principle Management Ltd; Berkeley Library, Trinity College Dublin; Blackrock Library, Co. Dublin; Bord Luthcleas Na hÉireann; Edward and Miriam Bourke; Margaret Brehon; Margaret Brittain; Donie Butler, Football Association of Ireland; Mary Carew, Fianna Fáil Press Office; Síle Carney, Knock Shrine; Castlebar Library, Co. Mayo; Central Library, ILAC Centre, Dublin; Anne Chambers; Margaret Chambers; Eamonn Coghlan; Maura Connolly, Late Late Show; Shaun Davey; Ronnie Delany; Dun Laoghaire Library, Co. Dublin; Brendan Dunne; Claire Fallon, Leinster House; Rev. Fr Farraher, Blackrock College; Anne Gannon; Frank Grealy, Irish runner; Mairéad Green; Marjorie Harding; Teri Hayden, The Agency; Frank Heneghan, College of Music; Mary Hickey, The Arts Council; Howth Library, Co. Dublin; Irish Film Board; Rev. Fr Colm Kilcoyne; Pauline McAlester, Murray Consultants; Jim McArdle, *The Irish Times*; Danny McGinley; Tom McGinty; Séamus MacMathuna, Comhaltas Ceoltóirí Éireann; Paddy Moloney; Patricia Moloney, Central Bank; Síle Mooney; Gabrielle Noble; Anne Nolan, Amnesty International; Séamas and Deirdre Ó Brógáin; Anna B. O'Connor, Concilium Legionis Mariae; Michael O'Donnell; RTE; Roberta Reeners, Editorial Consultant; Marie Rooney, Gate Theatre; Bride Rosney, Áras an Uachtaráin; Bridget Ryan, *The Irish Catholic*; Deirdre Ryan, Office of the Taoiseach; Jonathan Stephenson, SDLP Press Office; Maureen Storey, College of Music; Carole Sweetman, Olympia Theatre; Jillian Tynan; Toni Wall, Hatch Entertainments; Eleanor and Marie Therese Ward; Westport Library, Co. Mayo; Dr T. K. Whitaker

The author and publishers wish to thank the following sources for permission to reproduce photographs: Abbey Theatre; Liam de Paor; G. A. Duncan; Gallery Press; Nicola Gordon Bowe; Hulton-Deutsch; Illustrated London News; Independent Newspapers; Inpho; Irish Times; Tom Kennedy/Source; Lensmen; Mansell Collection Ltd; Murray Consultants; National Gallery of Ireland; National Library of Ireland; National Museum of Ireland; Br Nolan, O'Connell's Schools; Pacemaker; Maureen Potter; Press 22, Limerick; RTE; Sisters of Charity; Colin Smythe; Tara Records Ltd; UPI

(1787-1858)

Mary Aikenhead was born on 19 January 1787 in Cork. She was the eldest daughter of Dr and Mrs David Aikenhead. Mary's mother was a Catholic but her father was of Scottish Protestant descent. He was sympathetic to many of Ireland's problems, but not to the Catholic faith. At the time of their marriage, Mary's parents agreed that their children would be brought up as Protestants.

While Mary was still very young, Mrs Aikenhead persuaded the family doctor that their frail daughter needed fresh country air. The little girl was sent to the care of a Catholic family, the O'Rourkes, who lived outside the city. Mary lived with the O'Rourkes for six years and became one of the family. She prayed with them and attended Mass in their local church.

On her return to Cork, Mary attended a city school. However her earlier religious experiences with the O'Rourkes had left their mark. With the help of a friendly housemaid, Mary began to attend Mass secretly every morning before breakfast. In 1801, when Mary was fourteen, her father became very ill. He became a convert himself to Catholicism on his deathbed. In her sixteenth year, Mary also became a Catholic.

When she finished school, Mary could well have lived a life of ease in the rich society around her. However, she turned aside from the whirl of parties, balls and concerts, devoting her time and energy to the poor of Cork. After the death of her mother, Archbishop Murray of Dublin convinced her to set up a community of Irish Sisters of Charity. Mary then went to a convent in York with a companion where they remained as novices for three years. On their return to Dublin in September 1815, the women pronounced their vows to the bishop and opened their first convent in North William Street, Dublin. Mary was made Superior General of the Order, which was dedicated to teaching, caring for the sick, the poor and prisoners.

With cholera a constant menace in Dublin and Cork, the Sisters of Charity performed heroic work by nursing those who were seriously ill. Mary was shocked by the terrible scenes that met her eyes in the poorer city slums during the cholera epidemic of 1832. This led her to build a hospital for the Catholic poor in Dublin. She appealed everywhere for funds and a building at 56 St Stephen's Green was eventually purchased.

On 23 January 1834, although as yet without equipment, St Vincent's Hospital was born. It was the first hospital in Ireland to be served by nuns. From the beginning, Mother Mary was aware that her nurses should be well trained. Initially, her first nun-nurses were trained in Paris. But later, St Vincent's Hospital Nursing School became internationally famous. In 1970, St Vincent's Hospital moved to its present location, Elm Park, Merrion Road.

For the last three decades of her life, trouble with her spine confined Mary to a wheelchair and couch. But ill health did not quench her spirit and energy. She continued in her efforts at fundraising, administration and social reform and established ten convents of the Sisters of Charity Order in Ireland. In time, her sisters established roots all over the world. Mother Mary Aikenhead also founded the Hospice at Harold's Cross, where she herself died in 1858. Her coffin was carried to the grave in St Mary Magdalen's Cemetery in Donnybrook by Dublin working men. Later that year, the government issued a stamp in her honour, the first woman to receive such recognition. In 1921, Pope Benedict XV signed the decree for her beatification. This was a testimony to Mother Mary Aikenhead's unceasing efforts for the poor and sick.

An African girls' school run by the Sisters of Charity

MARY AIKENHEAD

(1922-1987)

Éamonn Andrews was born on 19 December 1922 in Synge Street, Dublin. He attended Holy Faith Convent in the Liberties before enrolling at the Synge Street Christian Brothers School. To protect himself against school bullies, he decided to join a local boxing club in York Street. His boxing career matured and he won the Irish Junior Middleweight title in 1944. Although interested in journalism, he accepted a job as clerk with the Hibernian Insurance Company in Dame Street, Dublin. But boredom drove him to seek a job in Radio Éireann as a part-time boxing commentator. Éamonn also contributed articles to boxing magazines and wrote a play entitled *The Moon is Black*, a comedy about a man who mistakenly thinks

he is a murderer. In 1946, he left insurance to become a freelance broadcaster. He was the host of Radio Éireann's most popular light entertainment show, 'Question Time'. On 'Microphone Parade', he interviewed celebrity guests, as well as presenting a quiz-cum-variety show, 'Double or Nothing'. Even at this early stage, Éamonn had the rare quality of being able to communicate easily with his audiences.

Moving to London, he presented the zany 'Ignorance is Bliss' and then 'Sports Report', an exciting show which attracted millions of listeners. During this period, Éamonn continued to fly back to Ireland for his radio commentaries and to visit Grainne Bourke who became his wife in 1951.

Éamonn Andrews' big break came as presenter of the popular TV show, 'What's My Line'. His professionalism and pleasant screen personality received widespread acclaim and the show fascinated viewers by introducing people working in all kinds of jobs. In July 1955, the BBC introduced its own version of an American TV show called 'This Is Your Life'. Éamonn was chosen as presenter. Although sentimental, the programme was a huge popular success. The first subject chosen to receive the now-famous red book was, to his total surprise, none other than Éamonn himself. The show was a firm favourite running for many years. It owed much of its success to its presenter, as well as to its element of surprise and to the variety of personalities featured.

During this period, Éamonn's boxing commentaries were, for millions of people, an essential part of 'World Title' nights. At the time, he was also doing a children's programme, 'Crackerjack', on which he showed his ease in dealing with youngsters, and a late-night Saturday radio chat show, 'Pied Piper'.

Incredibly, Éamonn also found time to develop his business interests in Ireland. He set up the Éamonn Andrews Studios, which produced sponsored programmes for Radio Éireann and he managed Dublin's Gaiety Theatre. His services to broadcasting were recognised when he was made chairman of the new Radio Telefís Éireann authority, through which he made a valuable contribution to the fledgling television system in Ireland.

Éamonn won the top television personality award in 1956 and 1957. He was now at the height of his career, earning more than any other TV performer. In 1964, he presented Britain's first television chat show, the 'Éamonn Andrews Show'. In the same year, he was made a Knight of St Gregory for his charitable work.

In 1970, Éamonn was granted an OBE (the Order of the British Empire), an unusual award for an Irish citizen. By now he was also fronting a new magazine programme on Thames Television, 'Today'. He hosted 'Time for Business', a programme which aimed to remove some of the mystery surrounding finance, and a late-night quiz show, 'Top of the World', which linked contestants in England, US and Australia by satellite.

Although his business interests slumped in Ireland due to a recession, Éamonn's success in England continued when 'What's My Line' was revived in 1984. However, his demanding work schedule and constant commuting put a strain on his heart. Following a collapse on the set of 'What's My Line', he died on 5 November 1987.

(1906-1989)

Samuel Barclay Beckett was born in Foxrock, Dublin, on 13 April 1906. He was the second son of William Beckett, a building contractor, and Mary Beckett, a former nurse.

After attending Earlsfort House School in Dublin, he was sent as a boarder to Portora Royal School in Enniskillen. While there he developed a keen interest in cricket and rugby, playing on school teams in both games. At seventeen, Beckett entered Trinity College, Dublin, where he studied English, French and Italian. He received his Bachelor of Arts degree in 1927, and a gold medal for outstanding performances in his final exams. He then taught for two terms in Belfast before leaving for Paris in October 1928.

In Paris, Beckett became a lecturer in English where he met another famous Irish writer, James Joyce. They shared an interest in experimental literary forms, an irreverent wit and a love-hate relationship with Ireland. Beckett wrote the French translation of the 'Anna Livia Plurabelle' section of Joyce's *Finnegans Wake*. He was then invited to contribute to a collection of essays written by Joyce's followers to defend their master's work.

In 1929, Beckett published his first mature work of fiction, *Assumption*, and his first literary criticism, *Dante . . . Bruno, Vico . . . Joyce*, which traces Joyce's reference to key Italian writers. The following year, Beckett's poem on Descartes, entitled 'Whoroscope', won the Nancy Cunard prize from Hours Press. He returned to Dublin in September, becoming Assistant in French at Trinity. He took his Masters Degree in 1931. By 1932, Beckett had resigned from lecturing in Trinity and embarked on a five-year tour of Germany, France, England and Ireland. His story, *Dante and the Lobster*, was published in 1932. It displays many marks of his subsequent works—the control and simplicity of language, and the use of wit, compassion and despair. In 1933, Beckett's father died, leaving him a yearly allowance of £200, a great deal of money at the time. In 1934, a book of stories called *More Pricks than Kicks* was published in London. It received a lukewarm reception, as did an undistinguished volume of poems, *Echo's Bones*. During the 1930s, Beckett's relationship with Joyce deepened and he was much involved in the Joyce circle.

In 1938, Beckett's first novel, *Murphy*, was published. It is a darkly comic protrayal of an idle, poverty-stricken scholar, overeducated to the point of despair. In the same year, Beckett was attacked and stabbed in the street and came close to death. During World War II (1939–45), he went 'underground' to serve with the French Resistance, preparing information on troop movements for microfilming. He was awarded France's special prize for bravery, the Croix de Guerre. His name was as yet comparatively unknown in the literary field—when he published his own French translation of *Murphy*, only ninety-five copies were sold in the first four years! Fleeing from the Gestapo with Suzanne Dumesnil (later his wife), Beckett settled in Rousillon where he began working on his novel, *Watt*. It was finished in 1945 but not published until 1953. He also enlisted for a while as a Red Cross volunteer.

The decade following the end of World War II was a period of intense creativity. In these years, Beckett wrote only in French. By 1955 his trilogy, *Molloy* (1951), *Malone dies* (1951) and *The Unnamable* (1953), had appeared, as well as *Mercier et Camier*. In less than six years, Beckett had written far more than during the previous sixteen. In 1952, his international reputation was established with his play, *Waiting for Godot*. In the years after its first production (Paris 1953), it became a spectacular worldwide success of post-war theatre. *Endgame*, Beckett's next play, was given its world première in London on 3 April 1957.

Krapp's Last Tape followed in 1958. Beckett's increasing reputation in England led to a series of commissions from the BBC, including *All That Fall* (broadcast 13 January 1957) and *Embers* (28 October 1959). Beckett returned to the novel in 1961 with *How It Is*. In *Happy Days* (1961), Winnie prattles on under a scorching sun while the sand rises towards her mouth, Beckett's merciless metaphor for man's condition. In 1966 *Eh Joe* was screened on BBC. In 1969, he was awarded the Nobel Prize for Literature. But, as ever shunning publicity, he refused to attend the prize-giving ceremony.

Later works included *Breath* (1969), *Not I* (1972), *That Time* (1976), *Footfalls* (1976), *Ghost Trio and . . . but the clouds* (1977), *Company* (1979), *A Piece of Monologue* (1979), *Mal Vu Mal Dit* (1981), *Rockaby* (1981), *Quad* (1981), *Catastrophe* (1982), *Worstward Ho* (1983), *Disjecta* (1983) and *What Where* (1983).

Samuel Beckett, one of Ireland's most famous literary exiles, died in Paris on 22 December 1989.

SAMUEL BECKETT

Brendan Behan was born on 9 February 1923, just as the Civil War (1922–23) was nearing its end. He was the first child of Stephen and Kathleen Behan. He was educated by the French Sisters of Charity, William Street, and later by the Christian Brothers at Brunswick Street. At fourteen he left school, taking up his father's trade of painting.

Behan's family was intensely Republican and the youngster was familiar with patriotic songs and stories from an early age. His father had been in prison for Republican activities, so it was not surprising, therefore, when Behan eventually joined the IRA. He was trained in the use of explosives as part of a campaign launched in England. In 1939, when he was just sixteen, he was arrested in Liverpool on a charge of possessing explosives. He was sentenced to three years' borstal detention, the maximum sentence that could be given to a juvenile.

After serving almost two years, Behan was released. Following his return to Dublin, however, he was rearrested in April 1942, charged with firing at a detective. Considered lucky to escape the death penalty, he was given a fourteen-year prison sentence. During his imprisonment, Brendan learned Irish and read widely in the libraries of Mountjoy Jail, Arbour Hill and the Curragh. He gained a vast knowledge of Irish history and of Irish and English literature. His story, 'How I became a Borstal Boy', was published in the influential magazine, *The Bell*, in 1942. Prison life supplied much of the raw material for his major works in the years ahead.

Fortune swung his way in 1946, when Behan benefited from a general amnesty. Following a period of travel punctuated by further short prison spells, Brendan settled in Dublin. He became a well-known character around Dublin streets and pubs and was a regular contributor of articles and stories to radio, magazines and newspapers. In December 1946, his first poem in Irish in honour of an IRA leader who died on hunger strike was published in an Irish magazine, *Comhar*. In 1954, *The Quare Fellow*, Behan's play about hanging, was staged in the small Pike Theatre, Dublin. A London production two years later gave his name wider recognition. By now he had married Beatrice Salkeld, the daughter of an artist. His play, *The Big House*, commissioned by the BBC, was broadcast in 1957. His play, *An Giall*, was first produced in 1958 at the Damer Irish language theatre. An English version, *The Hostage*, considerably developed the original script and had a very successful run soon after.

During the 1950s, Behan also wrote popular short stories such as *A Woman of No Standing*, *After The Wake* and *The Confirmation Suit*. He also wrote plays for radio including *Moving Out* and *A Garden Party*.

In October 1958, his novel, *Borstal Boy*, became a phenomenal success. This creative autobiography was a frank portrait of the artist as a young prisoner. Behan was now a celebrity whose colourful personality made him a popular guest on television and radio programmes. Productions of *The Quare Fellow* in New York, Paris and Berlin further strengthened his reputation. A crime story, serialised in *The Irish Times* in 1953, was published in 1964 as a book, *The Scarperer*.

Later books such as *Brendan Behan's Ireland*, *Brendan Behan's New York* and *Confessions of an Irish Rebel* display his characteristic humour. By now, however, he was a prisoner of his own success. Behan the writer was being overshadowed by Behan the drunkard. Under the strain of heavy drinking and diabetes, his health began to give way. The quality of his writing deteriorated with his failing health. He died in the Meath Hospital, Dublin, on 20 March 1964. Brendan Behan was buried in Glasnevin Cemetery

after a huge funeral which showed the affection for the 'Quare Fellow' held by the people of Dublin.

(1946-)

George Best was born on 22 May 1946 in east Belfast. As a young lad, he received his earliest coaching from his father who had him kicking a ball soon after the child could toddle. His mother, a keen hockey player, was also interested in sport.

When Best was fifteen, Manchester United's Belfast scout, Bob Bishop, recognised the boy's skill and potential. Bishop sent him to Manchester for a trial, but the slim youngster became homesick and ran back to Belfast.

The Manchester United manager, Matt Busby, eventually persuaded Best to remain at Old Trafford, one of soccer's best-known football grounds. At seventeen, Best made his début for the United first team against West Bromwich Albion in September 1963. Playing with him in the club's famous red strip were exciting footballers like Scotland's Denis Law and England's Bobby Charlton as well as other famous soccer names such as Crerand, Stiles, Dunne, Herd, Stepney and Sadlier. Best soon settled into this great side, a difficult task especially as the Red Devils were coming to their peak. After just seven months of playing first-team club football, George Best earned his first full international cap for Northern Ireland, an indication of his talent.

Best soon became a sensation, attracting large crowds who flocked to see his stunning skills on the ball. Even in that star-studded team, the range of Best's abilities, his total control while at top speed, his amazing balance, his imagination and cheek, and of course the glorious goals he scored soon made him a celebrity. Matt Busby, although encouraging Best to work as a member of a team, gave him full rein to display his breath-taking skills, dribbling his way past defenders in confined spaces as if by magic.

Best soon experienced success with United, winning League Championship medals in 1965 and 1967. He was by now a tightly marked man in most matches. Desperate defenders often resorted to kicking, pushing and tripping when faced with Best's skill.

The highlight of Best's career came at Wembley Stadium in 1968 when his team won the European Cup, beating the Portuguese champions Benfica 4–1 after extra time. One of these goals was scored by Best who coolly rounded the goalkeeper before stroking the ball into an empty net. On that memorable night, Manchester United became the first English club to win the European Cup.

George had had a hugely successful year. He was selected as English and European Footballer of the Year (1968), as well as being the First Division's top goalscorer. He was continually in the headlines over the next five years because of his dazzling skills on the field and his controversial behaviour off it. Media pressure on the young man was intense, with every action of his personal life under public examination. This, as well as his heavy drinking, quick temper and undisciplined lifestyle, led to his downfall after ten glorious years during which he scored 361 goals for United and 37 for Northern Ireland.

The strain on Best was beginning to tell. During 1972, as United plunged to the bottom of the First Division, he went missing from the club several times. Eventually, after further disagreements, United put Best on the transfer list. Although Best returned to the club later under the managership of Tommy Docherty, he played only a few games for the Red Devils. Retiring in 1973, he came back to play for a string of other clubs, but the old magic now appeared only in brief flashes during these twilight years.

George Best will be remembered as the footballing wizard who was one of Manchester United's greatest stars. Unfortunately, his exquisite footwork was never seen in the World Cup, despite the many wonderful goals he scored for Northern Ireland. Although it is almost twenty years since football was graced by the unique talents of George Best, his name is still a common measure by which soccer skills are judged.

(1786-1875)

Charles Bianconi was born on 24 September 1786 at Tregelo in northern Italy. During his childhood he was a poor scholar, preferring horses to books. He left school at fifteen and crossed into Switzerland while working for an Italian print-seller named Faroni. After much further travelling, Bianconi eventually arrived in Dublin.

Bianconi's employer knew there was a demand for picture prints in Dublin's large townhouses. So he sent Bianconi out into the city streets selling engravings. The youngster did so well that Faroni let him travel around the country with large numbers of prints.

When his apprenticeship was completed, Bianconi set up his own business. He travelled to Thurles, Co. Tipperary, where he became friendly with a young priest named Theobald Mathew (who later became famous as the founder of the temperance movement).

In 1807, Bianconi opened a shop in Waterford where he sold prints and mirrors. Here, he made another staunch friend in Edmund Ignatius (cf.) Rice (founder of the Irish Christian Brothers) who persuaded him to go back to his studies. Over the next few years, Bianconi worked hard at his business and books. In 1809, he moved to Clonmel. The people there called him 'Brian Cooney' (which was how the Italian name sounded to them). Bianconi's business flourished and he made many friends, including Daniel O'Connell. He joined O'Connell's Catholic Association and was involved in organising election meetings for the Liberator.

At this time, the world of most Irish people was bounded by the distance they could walk because stage coaches were too expensive. In his travels, Bianconi noticed the poor state of transport and communication in the country. Roads were dreadful, many of them no more than dirt tracks. His chance to do something about this came in 1814. With the ending of the great Napoleonic Wars in Europe, horses were no longer needed for cavalry regiments, so the price of horses and grain fell. Bianconi bought a horse for £10, and on 6 July 1815, the first Bianconi coach ran the ten miles from Clonmel to Cahir and back at an average speed of 7½ miles per hour. It carried six passengers who sat back-to-back, facing outwards. The fare was 2*d* a mile. The new service was much cheaper than a stage coach and faster than canal barges. Although people were reluctant to use it at first, the idea of public transport soon grew popular. Bianconi soon extended his route to Limerick, Cashel and Thurles. His coaches became familiar sights in many counties, linking towns and villages which had never known public transport. They were given the nickname 'Bians'. After a while, the 'Bians' changed to four wheelers, carrying up to nineteen passengers and pulled by three or four horses.

In 1834, the first railway in Ireland was built, joining Dublin and Dun Laoghaire. Although he was worried, Bianconi knew it would take time for the railroads to cover the country and that his coaches could eventually connect with the rail system. By 1836, 'Bians' were covering over two thousand miles daily from their new headquarters in Clondalkin, Dublin.

Bianconi was elected Mayor of Clonmel in 1844 in recognition of his great work. In 1846 he purchased Longfield, a large house and estate near Clonmel. During the Famine (1845–49), he was a kind landlord. By 1857, 'Bians' were travelling 4,000 miles daily. Fifty years after his first coach took to the road, Bianconi retired after a driving accident. He spent the last years of his life at Longfield where he died on 22 September 1875. It is said that the sound of horses' hooves were heard outside the house when he died.

(1960-   )

Packie Bonner was born on 24 May 1960 in Culglass, a small village near Burtonport, Co. Donegal, a county rich in soccer tradition. Both Packie and his twin brother, Denis, showed early potential in Gaelic football as well as in soccer. They received great encouragement from their builder father, Andrew. Manus McCole, manager of the local soccer team, Keadue Rovers, noticed Packie's abilities. He included Packie on the under-16 team, playing the fourteen-year old in an outfield position at first. Before long, however, Packie's exceptional goalkeeping skills came to the fore—the youngster had found his niche between the posts. The tall goalkeeper moved on to the Rovers senior team and eventually was included in the Irish Youth team. Packie also continued playing Gaelic football at centre-forward on Donegal's Minor team in the Ulster Championships of 1977.

Approached by Glasgow Celtic and given two trials with Leicester City, Packie eventually joined the Scottish club (which has had a traditional link with Donegal) at the age of eighteen. His name was the last to be signed by the legendary Glasgow Celtic manager, Jock Stein. The 6' 3" keeper made his début in the cauldron of the Scottish League on St Patrick's Day 1979. The 2–1 win over Motherwell was a favourable start to a marvellous career.

As the months went by, the genial Donegal man endeared himself to the Glasgow fans, who are notoriously difficult to impress. He soon established himself as the club's first-choice goalkeeper. His professionalism, sharp reflexes and absolute concentration during a game kept him guarding the Celtic net for twelve consecutive years. During this time he collected Scottish League medals, Scottish Cup-Final medals and League Cup medals with his club. Now a local hero, he lives in Glasgow with his Scottish wife, Ann, and their children.

Packie received his first international cap against Poland in May 1981—it was his 21st birthday. Before long, he had established himself as Ireland's regular last line of defence. Under the guidance of manager Jack Charlton from 1986 onwards, Packie was central in Ireland's qualification for the European Championship in Germany in 1988. On the run-in to that competition,

Ireland achieved a record of twelve games without defeat, an achievement in which Bonner's large hands played a major role. In June 1990, he was the national goalkeeper during the Republic of Ireland's historic participation in the World Cup Finals in Italy, the first time Ireland had qualified.

The overall performance of the Irish World Cup squad enthralled the nation. Following three drawn games—one-all against England, nil-all against Egypt and one-all against the Netherlands—Ireland was drawn against Romania in the second round. In a tense match, Bonner made the save of the game in the seventieth minute. After extra time, when the teams were still scoreless, the outcome was determined by penalties. Although Bonner anticipated the first four Romanian penalties, diving the correct way each time, there were no misses. With Sheedy, Houghton, Townsend and Cascarino replying for Ireland, the score after eight attempts stood at four goals each. Millions of Irish people held their breath as Bonner faced the fifth Romanian penalty taker. Reading the shot correctly, he spread himself to the right and parried the shot, punching the ground in delight. This crucial save gave the last Irish penalty-taker, David O'Leary, the chance to put Ireland into the quarterfinals of the World Cup against the host nation, Italy, in Rome. O'Leary, the big defender, put the ball into the net. Although Ireland was to lose 1–0 against the Italians, Bonner's inspiring performances throughout the campaign made him a national hero.

With over fifty international caps already to his credit, his steadying influence, unwavering concentration and agile reflexes look set to keep Packie Bonner minding the Irish net for some time to come.

(1960-   )

Paul David Hewson is better known as the singer, Bono. He was born on 10 May 1960 in Ballymun, Dublin, and was educated at Mount Temple Comprehensive School. The second son of an interdenominational marriage, he enjoyed a quiet family life until his mother's tragic death in 1975. The young teenager went through a rebellious phase, roaming the streets. However, music was to provide an outlet for him. Learning that a school friend, Larry Mullen, was attempting to form a band, Paul decided to join. The other members of the group were Adam Clayton and David Evans (known as 'The Edge'). Paul Hewson called himself 'Bono', while the band was known as U2. Concentrating on building up experience,

they tried to break into the local music scene. Bono was now more determined than ever to build a career in music since his application to University College, Dublin, had been rejected because he lacked the necessary qualifications in Irish.

As winners of a national talent competition, U2 came to the attention of Paul McGuinness early in 1978. Impressed by U2's commitment and Bono's direct relationship with audiences, he became their manager. In December 1979, U2 played concerts in London, having earlier released their first record, 'U23', which attracted a positive critical response.

January 1980 saw U2 win five awards. They signed up with Island Records and released their début album, *Boy*, and three singles. They also completed a tour of Britain with more concerts in Belgium and Holland. New horizons were charted with their first American tour.

In October 1981, U2's second album, *October*, entered the UK charts at No. 11 and earned the group their first silver disc. The following month the band returned to America for the *October* tour. In March 1982, the year during which Bono married his childhood sweetheart, Alison, their third single, 'A Celebration', was released. They were now a disciplined band, with Bono's voice developing in power and expressiveness. Following the release of the single, 'New Year's Day', in January 1983, the album, *War*, entered the charts at No. 10.

Further successes followed: their first American gold disc (April 1983); 'A Day at the Races' concert in Dublin's Phoenix

Park (August 1983); a Japanese tour (November 1983); a platinum disc for the single 'A Blood Red Sky' (January 1984); 1983 Band of the Year; a world tour; a silver disc for the single, 'Pride (In the Name of Love)'; and No. 1 for *The Unforgettable Fire* (October 1984), an album whose title came from a series of paintings by survivors of the Japanese nuclear holocaust in 1945.

Following a concert in Dublin's Croke Park, U2 played their part in the Live Aid Concert in July 1985 to raise money for famine relief in Africa. In 1986, they played Dublin's Self-Aid concert to benefit Ireland's unemployed. They produced the album, *The Joshua Tree* (March 1987), the fastest selling album in British music history, and closed a European tour with an open-air concert in Cork (August 1987).

In 1988, U2 won two Grammy Awards, Album of the Year for *The Joshua Tree* and Best Rock Performance with the single, 'Desire'. The following year, U2 received an American Grammy for Best Performance and Best Video (for the single, 'Where the Streets have No Name'). A new-year show that year transmitted by RTE and BBC reached an audience of 500 million. In January 1990, U2 were nominated for Grammy Awards in two categories: Best Rock Performance ('When Love Comes to Town') and Best Song written for a Motion Picture ('Angel of Harem').

Although the band spends much time touring abroad, Bono and his col-

leagues record in Dublin, employing many Irish people in their vast entourage. Bono's social concern has seen them interrupt profitable schedules for fundraising ventures such as Amnesty, Aids and Artists Against Apartheid. In 1991, an album, *Achtung Baby*, was released, followed by another sell-out American tour.

BONO (PAUL HEWSON)

(c.940-1014)

Brian MacKennedy, better known as Brian Bórú, was born around the year 940. He was the youngest son of Cennetig who ruled the small Dál Cais kingdom in east Clare. Brian became King of Munster in 978 after his brother, Mathgamhain, was killed in an ambush. He then set out to control the warlike Norsemen who lived in the area.

Brian was a clever general who liked to work out his battle tactics in advance. From his base at Kincora near Lough Derg (now Killaloe, Co. Clare), he used his forces, both army and navy, to great effect. By 984, he had won the kingship of most of Leinster and Munster. Brian had hundreds of ships under his command with which he controlled the entire length of the Shannon.

When Mael Sechnaill became High King of Tara in 980, a power struggle developed between the two about who should rule Ireland. In 997, Brian and Mael Sechnaill reached a compromise and agreed to share the country between them. As a result, Brian took Munster and Dublin, while Mael Sechnaill ruled the rest. Before long, trouble erupted again after Mael Sechnaill's brother-in-law joined with Sitric, King of Dublin, against Brian. Brian reacted swiftly. Gathering his army, he marched eastwards from Kincora. Just outside Dublin, Brian's forces defeated the rebel army.

Meanwhile, the fragile peace between Mael Sechnaill and Brian was shattered when, in a battle to claim the High Kingship, Brian's army was defeated at Tara. After this, Brian decided it was wise to return home. Having reorganised his forces, Brian sailed his fleet up the Shannon. Marching on Athlone, he forced Mael Sechnaill to surrender. Brian, now in his sixties, had at last become High King of Ireland.

Brian's first years in power were peaceful but busy. He toured the entire country, meeting the local chieftains. He often collected cows as a form of tax. This practice earned him his nickname, Brian Bórú (Boruimhe), Brian of the Tributes. But he was growing old. His enemies, forever watchful, thought that Brian's control might be slipping. Once again, Sitric's Norsemen joined with the Leinstermen and attacked Malachy, who governed the northern part of Ireland for Brian. Brian immediately sent help. But after besieging Dublin for a number of months in 1013, he returned to Kincora.

Meanwhile, Sitric sent messages to Scotland and to the Isle of Man for Viking reinforcements. Two thousand Viking soldiers answered the call to arms. Brian was joined by armies from Connacht and Munster, as well as Malachy's soldiers. The two sides faced each other across the sandy plain of Clontarf, near Dublin, on Good Friday, 23 April 1014.

After a long, furious battle the Norsemen retreated. Many of them drowned in the high tide as they tried to reach their ships. However, Brian's day of glory ended tragically. One of the retreat-ing Norsemen, Broder, happened by chance to see Brian alone in his tent, praying for success. The elderly king was not strong enough to take part in the battle himself. Broder entered the tent and killed him with an axe.

So victory was soured with sadness. In the battle Brian's son and grandson were also killed. After the Battle of Clontarf, however, Norsemen in Ireland were a faded force, no longer capable of taking over the country. Most of them settled down to live peaceful lives in Ireland. Brian Bórú, High King of Ireland, is said to have been buried amid great ceremony at Armagh Cathedral.

Much of the life of St Brendan the Navigator is known only through legend. The son of Finlogue, he was probably born near Tralee, Co. Kerry, sometime around the year 486. He was baptised by a local bishop called Erc. Brendan was fostered at a monastery in Co. Limerick for five years. It was here that he received his education from Irish and Welsh saints. After studying under Finian of Clonard, Jarlath of Tuam and Enda of Aran, Brendan was ordained by Erc and was later made an abbot. His most important monastic foundations were at Clonfert, Co. Galway, Annadown, Co. Galway, and Ardfert, Co. Kerry. In all of these monasteries, Brendan laid down very strict rules for his monks.

In the tradition of many Irish missionaries, Brendan was a great traveller.

Many places, including Mount Brandon in Co. Kerry and Brandenburg in Germany, are said to have been named in his honour. Brendan visited Brittany in France as a missionary between 520 and 530. He is said to have journeyed to Scotland as well where he held an important conference with St Columba. His many voyages earned him the name of Brendan the Navigator. The famous story of his epic voyage across the western sea is told in a medieval book, *Navigatio Sancti Brendani* (the *Voyage of Brendan*). It was translated into many European languages during the Middle Ages. In it, Brendan's journey to the Isle of Blest is narrated. Many historians believe this was America. So was Brendan the first person from Europe to land in the New World? To find out if this could be true, the modern-day explorer, Tim Severin, decided to retrace Brendan's voyage. He was guided by the clues found in the original book. Severin also used the same type of boat and supplies mentioned by Brendan.

The *Navigatio* included a description of a burning island. Severin decided this must have been one of the volcanic islands off Iceland. Land that moved under the saint's boat could have been caused by the movement of whales which were attracted to the leather craft, Severin argued. A huge sheet of glass appeared in the sea, to Brendan's amazement. Severin said this could well have been one of the floating glaciers which are found in the North Atlantic.

After many adventures and near misses, Tim Severin and his crew arrived in their leather-covered boat on the coast of

Newfoundland. They proved that Brendan the Navigator and his fellow monks could well have been the first European people to set foot on American soil, centuries before the Vikings and almost a thousand years before Christopher Columbus.

In his old age, Brendan visited the great missionary, Columba. He died when he was over 90 years of age and is regarded as the patron saint of sailors and travellers. He was buried at Clonfert. His feast day is on 16 May, a day on which many pilgrims still climb to the summit of Co. Kerry's Mount Brandon.

(1852-1932)

Louis Brennan was born in Castlebar, Co. Mayo, on 28 January 1852. He was the son of a hardware merchant in the town. At that time, lack of employment forced many Irish people to emigrate in search of better opportunities. The Brennans left to seek their fortune in Australia when Louis was nine.

During his childhood, Louis Brennan was fascinated by machines and puzzles. After a few years' schooling, he had already invented rough models of an incubator, a safety window catch and a weighing machine, among others. When his schooling was over, he worked for a while as a watchmaker.

Later, Brennan became aware of the cost and difficulties of building railway lines over mountainous land. He then began to work at developing a vehicle which, although moving on a single line, would remain upright even when travelling round sharp corners. This invention, which would greatly reduce the costs of railway track construction, was called the gyrostat monorail, or gyrocar.

In 1874, Brennan designed the dirigible torpedo, the most successful of his many extraordinary inventions. Four years later he received his patent—the vital document which gives an inventor the sole right of selling a design. The British government was interested in the military possibilities of the torpedo. They bought the invention from Brennan for £100,000. Brennan was appointed superintendent at the government factory in Gillingham where his torpedo was manufactured. He later became consultant engineer.

1892 was a happy year for Brennan. He married Anna Quinn and bought Woodlands, a large house standing on twelve acres near Gillingham in Kent. From there he experimented with new inventions. After a world première demonstration of his full-size car in 1909, the invention won first prize at the Japanese-British Exhibition in 1910.

Brennan worked for the British government Ministry of Munitions before and after World War I. He developed Brennan's Flying Machine—the helicopter. However, despite government interest, the money needed to develop the project was withdrawn. This prevented him from being acknowledged as the designer of the first helicopter in general use.

Brennan was not a man to let disappointment halt him in his tracks. He kept himself busy producing a gyrocar. Although it attracted great attention from the leading car manufacturers of the time, it was never developed. This invention and the Brennangraph, a small machine for note-taking, were never commercially produced until many years later.

Recovering from illness in Montreux, in France, Louis Brennan, inventor of the safe gyrocar, was knocked down by a car and died of his injuries in January 1932. He was buried in London.

(452-c.525)

Facts about the life of St Brigid are few. Much of our knowledge of her comes through stories of miracles, many of which are deeply rooted in Irish folklore. Some sources say that Brigid came from Kildare. But she was probably born at Faughert, near Dundalk, Co. Louth, and baptised by St Patrick. Brigid's earliest biographers wrote about her more than a hundred years after her death. They state that her father was Dubthach, a powerful pagan nobleman of Leinster. However, there is little agreement about her mother, Brocassa. Some claim that she was of noble blood. Others say that she was a beautiful slave girl in Dubthach's household. Brigid is said to have spent her early years with a Druid to whom she may

have been sent in fosterage, the old Gaelic method of education.

Although her father selected a man of high rank (a poet) to marry his daughter, Brigid decided to follow a religious life. Along with seven other girls, all dressed in homespun white wool, she made her sacred vows. By so doing, they had started the first official community of nuns in Ireland. Brigid did not see the role of a nun as living apart from the world in cloistered seclusion. Instead, she travelled widely, organising convents, meeting great chieftains, visiting the poor and lonely on foot and by chariot. She also brought medical attention to the sick. Brigid's most famous convent, which became the headquarters of her mission, was at Kildare. It was marked by a large oak tree which inspired the place name, Kildare (*Cill Dara*), Church of the Oaks. Kildare ranked with the greatest of the monastic centres in Ireland. It had two separate cloisters side by side, one for the nuns, the other for monks.

According to the legends, Brigid's charity to the poor was limitless. It is said that she handed over her father's treasured sword to a poor man. The dinner which she and her nuns had prepared for important guests was served instead to beggars who called at the convent gate. Miracles attributed to her include the multiplication of food and the changing of water into beer. It was said that her cows gave milk three times daily, which is why Brigid is the patron saint of dairying. She is also the special saint of students, poets, blacksmiths and healers. In her lifetime, she was known for her efforts at securing the release of prisoners and hostages.

Irish missionaries carried her name throughout Europe from the sixth century onwards. One legend states that Brigid was the patron saint of the knights of chivalry who began the custom of calling the girls they married their 'brides' after her. Brigid's memory to this day is most especially celebrated in Ireland, where she is held in honour second only to St Patrick. The tradition of the special St Brigid's cross still remains. According to legend, the saint converted a pagan on his deathbed by plaiting rushes on the floor into the shape of the Cross at Calvary. This inspired the tradition of plaiting St Brigid's crosses.

On her death, in about 525, Brigid was at first laid to rest in her own church at Kildare in a casket of precious metals and jewels under a golden crown. Later, in 835, her remains were moved for safety during a period of Viking raids. Tradition states that, along with Patrick and Colmcille, she was reinterred in one grave at Downpatrick. A relic of her shoe, made of silver and brass, can be seen in the National Museum, Dublin. She was known as Mary of the Gael, the Queen of the South and the Prophetess of Christ. Many churches throughout Ireland are named after her. St Brigid's feast day is on 1 February, the first day of spring.

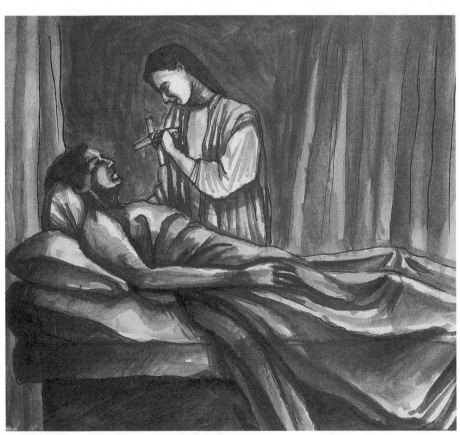

(1932-1981)

Christy Brown was born on 5 June 1932. He was the tenth of twenty-two children born to a bricklayer and his wife in Crumlin, Dublin. Thirteen of the Brown children survived to adulthood. Christy was unable to stand, walk or feed himself. His speech was barely comprehensible. For much of his early childhood, he was trundled around in a homemade box-cart.

Christy suffered from a form of cerebral palsy that left him with little control over any part of his body except for his left foot. Incredibly, using that foot, he succeeded in typing out an autobiography, several volumes of poetry and four novels.

Christy's mother resisted all attempts to have him sent to an institution. When her son was five, she discovered that he could grip a crayon between his toes. She taught him to write the alphabet and to read. His efforts were further guided by a Dublin pediatrician, Dr Robert Collis, who trained him to co-ordinate movement and speech.

Christy soon began to write in earnest, picking out the letters on a typewriter with the little toe of his left foot. Encouraged by Dr Collis, he wrote an account of his early childhood, *My Left Foot* (1954). In 1970 this was expanded into *Down All The Days*, an autobiographical novel about a poor Dublin family with a frustrated father who was often drunk and violent. The novel occupied him for ten years. It combined gritty realism with lyrical language in a rich mosaic of dreams and dreads. *Down All The Days* was a popular success in many languages, making Christy financially comfortable. In the following year, *Come Softly to My Wake*, his first volume of verse, also became a bestseller.

After the death of his mother in 1968, Christy was cared for by his sister. In 1972, he married Mary Carr, a nurse. The couple moved to Somerset in England where their house was outfitted with mechanical aids to give him improved independence of movement.

Down All The Days was eventually followed by two sequels—*A Shadow on Summer* (1974) and *Wild Grow the Lilies* (1976), and further volumes of poetry. In addition to writing, Christy also painted, holding the brush with his left foot. The proceeds from the sale of his artwork went to organisations working on behalf of disabled people.

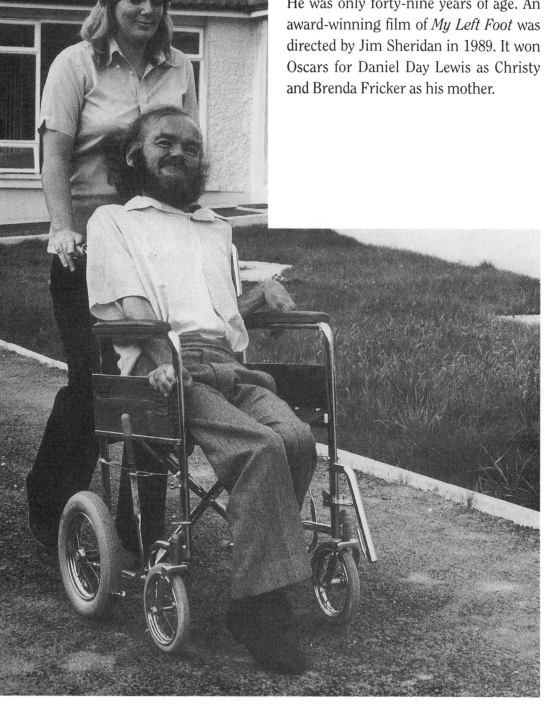

Delighting in lively company, Christy was a heavy drinker. His sudden death, after choking on food following sleeping tablets and drink, occurred at his home in Somerset on 6 September 1981. He was only forty-nine years of age. An award-winning film of *My Left Foot* was directed by Jim Sheridan in 1989. It won Oscars for Daniel Day Lewis as Christy and Brenda Fricker as his mother.

(1729-1797)

Edmund Burke was born at 12 Arran Quay, Dublin, on 12 January 1729. His father, a wealthy lawyer, joined the Anglican Church, but his mother was a Catholic. Although the boy was brought up as an Anglican, his mother's religion was to be a balancing influence on him in later life.

At first, Burke was educated at an open-air hedge school before moving to a Quaker school in Kildare. Graduating from Trinity College, Dublin, in 1748, he studied law at the Middle Temple in London. However, his interests were more literary and political than legal. This led him to write a famous political satire entitled *A Vindication of Natural Society* which was published in 1756. The following year, Burke married Jane Nugent, an Irish doctor's daughter. Although a Catholic, she converted to the Anglican Church. In 1759, Burke became first editor of the *Annual Register*, an influential world review of politics and economics. He supervised its production for almost thirty years.

In 1761, Burke was appointed private secretary to William Hamilton, the Chief Secretary in Ireland. After an argument, he left to serve as secretary to the Prime Minister, Lord Rockingham. In 1765, he was elected to the British parliament, where he served as a member of parliament for twenty-nine years. His literary interests were not forgotten, however, and he joined the famous Literary Club in London.

In parliament, Burke's powerful speeches stressed the need for moral solutions to political problems and raised the standard of parliamentary debate. Burke never hesitated to speak his mind, becoming involved in every major political issue of his time. In 1770 he wrote a pamphlet which defended individual liberty against King George III's efforts to strengthen the monarchy's power. Burke appealed for fair treatment of the American colonists. He campaigned for better government in India, supported the civil rights of Catholics in Ireland and demanded the end of slave trading. In 1789, the French Revolution dominated European life. Although Burke had campaigned to lessen the power of monarchs, he spoke out against the violence and lawlessness in France in his famous book, *Reflections on the Revolution in France* (1790). He declared that the uncontrolled bloodshed could lead to a new tyranny. He also denounced the revolution's dismissal of individual rights and its threat to religion and social order.

On retiring from parliament in 1794, Burke turned his attention to Ireland. His son, Richard, was appointed Secretary to the Catholic Committee of Ireland for a short while, but he was a disappointment in the job and was soon replaced by Wolfe Tone. His sudden death in 1795 was a terrible blow to his father.

Burke's last writings—*Letters to a Noble Lord* (1798) and *Letters on a Regicide* (1796–97)—were powerful works displaying his persuasive abilities to the full.

Edmund Burke died on 9 July 1797 at his estate in Beaconsfield, England. By then, to his disappointment, Ireland was poised for rebellion. He will be remembered as a political philosopher whose thoughts are still important nearly two hundred years later.

Trinity College Dublin, where Burke was educated

(1820-1861)

Robert O'Hara Burke was born in 1820 in a townland between Craughwell and Loughrea in Co. Galway. Educated in Belgium, he decided to follow his father into a military career. In 1840, he enlisted in the Austrian Army, becoming a captain within a short time. In 1848, he came back to Ireland and joined the Irish Constabulary. Within five years, however, his restless nature brought him to Australia where he became Inspector of Police in the state of Victoria. When an expedition was organised to explore the Australian continent from south to north he was made leader, despite the fact that he was unfamiliar with the hot uninhabited areas of the outback. Money was raised and no trouble spared to equip the expedition. Over five

thousand pounds were spent importing camels from India. Burke's mission was to collect specimens of plants, rocks and other scientific information, but the ambition of his group was to be the first to cross the continent.

On 20 August 1860, the Victorian Expedition left Melbourne on their way north. Following an argument between Burke and a man named Landells, who was in charge of the camels, Landells deserted the group in October. On 11 November, an advance party led by Burke arrived at Cooper's Creek where they waited for the rest of the party. Burke knew that 500 miles of unexplored land lay ahead. When the rearguard had not arrived by 16 December, Burke decided to set out on the last section of the crossing without them. With three companions— Wills, Gray and King—six camels, one horse and three months' supply of food, he left Cooper's Creek for the Gulf of Carpentaria. They left an assistant named Brahe behind, telling him to wait there for three months. Brahe was to head home if Burke's party had not returned by then. Under the circumstances, Burke decided not to bring any scientific equipment, losing the opportunity for gathering any useful information.

None of the group had any experience travelling through the dangerous country that lay ahead. Although it was the middle of Australia's summer, Burke was relieved to find that an unusual wet spell meant there were ample supplies of water in creeks and ponds. They reached the estuary of the Flinders River in February 1861, becoming the first white people to cross the continent of Australia.

The return journey was not so smooth. Burke was weakened by dysentery after eating a snake. Gray became ill as well and died on 17 April. Four days later, the exhausted little group reached Cooper's Creek, expecting to be met by Brahe with life-saving supplies. Instead, a note told them that he had just set off for home, leaving them only a few provisions. After five days' rest at the creek, they set off again. On 28 April, one of their last two camels had to be shot. By 10 May, the last one was killed, forcing them to abandon their equipment.

The last entry in Wills's journal was for 26 June 1861. Two days later Burke, the leader of the group, died of starvation. The one survivor, King, was found and cared for by Aborigines before being rescued by a relief party in September. The bodies of Burke and Wills were taken back to Melbourne where they were buried after a public funeral. Robert O'Hara Burke had died because of misfortune and misjudgments, but his exploration opened up communications across some of the most treacherous country in the world.

ROBERT O'HARA BURKE

(1889-1958)

Margaret Burke-Sheridan was born in 1889 in Castlebar, Co. Mayo, where her father was postmaster. The youngest of five, her childhood was scored with sadness. When Margaret was only four, her mother died. This loss was followed by further upset when her brothers and sister emigrated to England and America. Left alone after her father's death in 1901, she was sent to Eccles Street Dominican School, Dublin, which became her home for eight years. Convent life must have been lonely for the orphan girl, especially during school holidays.

Margaret's talents were not neglected, however, as she was a fine singer. Her promising voice was trained by Mother Clement and later by Dr Vincent O'Brien, who also taught John McCormack and James Joyce. Margaret was awarded the Gold Medal at the 1908 Feis Ceoil in the mezzo-soprano category. After this, money was raised to send her to the Royal Academy of Music in London. A wealthy couple, Lord and Lady De Walden were entranced by the quality of Margaret's voice. They introduced this fresh new talent to fashionable London society.

Her warm voice, attractive looks and lively personality made quite an impression. However, her heart was in professional opera rather than in pleasant but unchallenging musical recitals. With Europe sliding towards war, this ambition seemed remote until luck changed the course of her life. An Irish-Italian, Marconi, inventor of the wireless, was so impressed by her that he brought her to Italy, the home of opera.

Marconi introduced Margaret to Martino, who accepted her as a pupil. Her operatic debut was sensational, with luck again playing its part. On 3 February 1918, Margaret replaced the ailing soprano, Bovi, as Mimi in Puccini's *La Bohème*. Margaret had only received four days' notice, yet she captivated the Roman audience at the Costanzi Opera. She enjoyed further success in Milan and Naples. 'La Sheridan' soon became popular in a country where foreign singers were seldom successful.

The famous composer, Puccini, came to hear her in *Madame Butterfly*. He was so impressed that he decided to coach her in *Manon Lescaut* (1923). He even presented Margaret with a magnificent costume of gold and blue silk to wear on opening night.

In 1922, Toscanini, director of the legendary La Scala Opera (Milan), chose her for several major roles. Margaret partnered the renowned Italian tenor, Gigli, in Rimini and enjoyed further successes in many Italian cities.

In 1929, she made the first complete recording of *Madame Butterfly* on HMV records. From 1923 to 1930, she represented La Scala at Covent Garden in London. But Margaret loved Italy and refused many attractive offers to sing in America.

If her entry on to the operatic stage was sudden, her exit was equally abrupt. A broken romance and medical problems resulted in a loss of self-confidence in her voice, and led to her early retirement. In 1950, her contribution to Ireland's musical history was recognised when she was appointed to the Advisory Committee of the American National Arts Foundation. She died of cancer on 16 April 1958 and was buried at Glasnevin Cemetery.

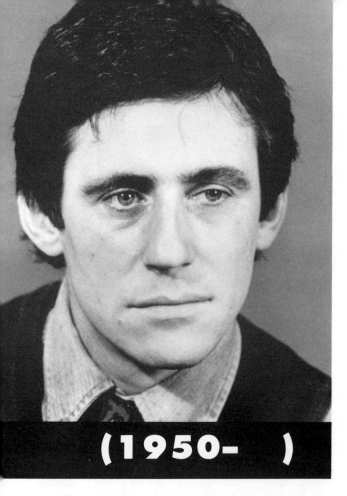

(1950-)

Gabriel Byrne was born in Walkinstown, Dublin, on 12 May 1950. He is the eldest in a family of six. His father Dan worked at Guinness's brewery and his mother Eileen was a nurse. As a boy, Gabriel learned to play the piano. He liked reading and was a clever mimic. Gabriel received his early education at Drimnagh Castle Christian Brothers School. Later, at St Richard's College, Worcester, England, he won a scholarship to UCD. This gave him the chance to study phonetics, languages and archaeology. During his student years, he broadcast short stories and verse on BBC and RTE and also edited a literary magazine. While working as a teacher of Irish and Spanish, he first stepped on the stage with the Dublin Shakespeare Society production of

Coriolanus in 1976. He also acted in various plays at Dublin's Focus Theatre.

Gabriel Byrne's professional acting career began in 1977 with *The Liberty Suit* by Mannix Flynn which was staged at the Project Theatre. After a number of roles in the Abbey Theatre he became nationally famous for his part in the television series 'The Riordans' (1978). In 1979, a spin-off series, 'Bracken', further boosted his reputation. This led to a minor part in John Boorman's version of the Arthurian legend, *Excalibur*, in 1980. This film début was followed by a series of well-received television costume epics for British and American networks. These included *Wagner* (London Films 1980); *Treatment* (BBC 1982); *Joyce in June* (produced by BBC for the 1982 Joyce centenary); *Christopher Columbus* (CBS 1983); and *Mussolini* (NBC 1984). Following *Excalibur*, he starred in films such as *The Search for Alexander the Great* (1981), *The Rocking Horse* (1982), *The Keep* (1982) and *Hannah K* (1983). Then came his fine cinema performance in the 1985 thriller, *Defence of the Realm*. Byrne's portrayal of an investigative journalist who disturbs the British establishment drew critical acclaim, as did his performances in *The Courier* (1987) and *A Soldier's Tale* (1987). However, his willingness to deviate from safe commercial roles has sometimes resulted in some unsuccessful ventures. During the filming of *Siesta* (1986) he played a romantic role with the American actress, Ellen Barkin, whom he later married. The couple have a young son, Jack, and live in New York.

After starring in *Hello Again* (1988) and *Diamond Skulls* (1989), Byrne's brooding presence as a dangerous, arrogant gangster in *Millers Crossing*, a witty, atmospheric thriller, was widely acknowledged as the most complex and well-developed performance of his first decade in film. It won critical acclaim and was named one of the top ten films of 1990. During the same year he also acted in *Shipwrecked* and recently, in a new departure, made a children's film, *Cool World*, with Disney. In *Into the Wind* (1991), a film shot in Connemara and Dublin, he played the part of Papa Reilly, once king of the gypsies but, since his wife's death, a shadow of his former self.

Byrne has continued writing, contributing over the years to *Magill*, *National Lampoon* and *Humor*. Future ambitions include a film which he is to produce, on the wrongful imprisonment of the Guildford Four. Byrne's intense screen presence, his powerful acting style and his current popularity indicate a bright cinematic future for this versatile Irish actor.

(1934-   )

Gay Byrne, Ireland's foremost broadcaster, was born in Rialto, Dublin, in 1934. Educated in Synge Street Christian Brothers School, he sampled various occupations in insurance, cinema management, car hire and advertising before finding fulfilment in broadcasting. He began his lengthy career with Radio Éireann in 1958. Over the years, he built up a faithful following in many sponsored radio programmes such as 'Jazz Corner' (reflecting his own love for such music) and 'Music on the Move'. For the last two decades, he has been associated with the hugely popular morning programme, the 'Gay Byrne Show'. Its mixture of comment, music and information on every possible issue has reflected the myriad changes in modern Irish society. In the role of presenter, he sifts, questions, teases and hectors, displaying a unique blend of professional and instinctive skills on the air. So successful was the programme's blend of content and style that it was extended to almost two hours daily.

Gay Byrne cut his television teeth with Granada TV, Manchester, where he appeared as newscaster, reporter and interviewer. Later he moved to London before a wider audience with BBC 2. With the advent of television in Ireland, he became a newscaster on RTE during its first year, and was the presenter of several successful shows such as 'Jackpot', 'Pick of the Pops', 'Film Night', 'Housewife of the Year', 'The Rose of Tralee' and the 'Telethon'. To millions of viewers he is, above all, known as producer and host of the top-rating 'Late Late Show' which has been on the air for three decades. Originally screened on Saturday, the programme moved to a Friday night slot in September 1985. The 'Late Late Show' started as a light summer magazine programme for a trial eight-week run in July 1962. It was such a phenomenal success that its run was extended to thirty-six weeks. The programme has become a forum for debate and entertainment, sometimes presenting controversial issues for discussion but also acquainting the nation with the cream of international but also Irish celebrities. The 'Late Late Show' is now a national institution, firmly stitched into the fabric of modern Irish life. It is the longest running live chat show with the same host in the world. Since November 1984, edited versions of 'The Late

Late Show' have been broadcast to British viewers on Channel 4 on Mondays.

In the summers of 1986 and 1987, Gay presented 'People are Talking', a TV programme for WBZ TV, Boston. In 1985, Gabbro Ltd, his own production company, produced and presented two documentaries for television, 'And Roses Grow There Now' and 'The Doctor Who Bought his Own Hospital'. Gabbro also produces staff-training video tapes.

Gay Byrne is the author of *To Whom It Concerns*, written to celebrate the first ten years of 'The Late Late Show'. His autobiography, *The Time of My Life* (written in collaboration with the journalist, Deirdre Purcell), was a bestseller in 1989. He has been a regular contributor to various newspapers and magazines, and has written a weekly column for the *Sunday World* newspaper since 1977.

Gay has received countless awards in recognition of his impressive contribution to broadcasting. These have included the Jacobs Awards, the Publicity Club of Ireland Award in 1986 and Entertainer of the Year in 1987 and 1988. He was also awarded an honorary Doctorate in Letters from Trinity College, Dublin, on 3 March 1988.

Gay Byrne is married to Kathleen Watkins, the well-known harpist, singer, ex-RTE continuity announcer and television presenter. They have two daughters. He lives in Howth where, along with a cottage in Donegal, he relaxes in relative privacy, enjoying cycling, walking, photography, piano playing, reading and a wide collection of jazz music. Fund-raising Chairman for the Irish Cancer Society and the Arthritis Association of Ireland, Gay Byrne's concern for the poor and neglected sections of society has been consistent throughout a distinguished career, resulting in some of the most moving interviews ever aired on radio or television.

(1670-1738)

Turlough Carolan was born in 1670 near Nobber, Co. Meath. His family moved to Roscommon where his father, who may have been a blacksmith, worked for the MacDermott Roe family ironworks at Alderford.

Mrs Mary MacDermott Roe looked after Turlough's education. But when he lost his eyesight from smallpox, she arranged for him to learn the harp. At this time music was a common occupation for the blind.

After three years spent learning the harp, Mrs MacDermott Roe provided him with a horse to bring him around the country. He was also given money and a servant. Although blind, Carolan loved laughter, good company and the pleasures of life. He was warmly received in the great houses where he received board and lodgings in return for playing. However, it was as a composer rather than as a musician that he made his name. Carolan wrote his lyrics in Irish. He often repaid hospitality by naming musical pieces after his benefactors—for example, 'Planxty Reynolds', 'Planxty Maguire' (a planxty is a tune for a harp). Carolan also composed Irish verse. His early training made him skilled at composition without having to write the material down.

An early love affair inspired the tune 'Bridget Cruise'. Incredibly, many years after they had parted, he was able to recognise his old love simply by the touch of her fingers when climbing into a boat on Lough Derg.

Italian music was popular at that time in Dublin, and Carolan's music was influenced by Italian composers such as Corelli, Vivaldi and Geminiani. In Dublin he was friendly with Jonathan Swift. Carolan travelled widely in Connacht and Ulster (his wife, Mary Maguire, came from Co. Fermanagh). He depended on the generosity of his patrons, returning often to houses where he had been made welcome before. Eventually he settled in Co. Leitrim with his wife and seven children. One of his laments was written after her death in 1733.

When Carolan himself felt death was approaching, he returned to his earliest home with the MacDermott Roe family, picked up his harp and played his 'Farewell to Music'. On his deathbed, he is supposed to have called for a cup of whiskey, but when it arrived, was unable to drink it. He then kissed the cup, saying that old friends should part with a kiss.

Carolan died at Alderford, Co. Roscommon, on 25 March 1738. His funeral was attended by a huge crowd, including harpers from all over Ireland. After a wake lasting four days, Carolan was buried at the MacDermott Roe family chapel in Kilronan. More than two hundred of Carolan's melodies have survived to this day.

Harry Clarke was born on 17 March 1889, at 33 North Frederick Street, Dublin. His English father, Joshua, had established his church decoration business at this address three years previously.

Educated at Belvedere College, young Harry began working in his father's studio at the age of sixteen. Under Joshua's guidance, Harry learned the basics of stained glass technique. At night he attended the Metropolitan School of Art where he became a full-time student in 1910. His talent in the medium of stained glass brought him to early prominence with a series of awards, including Gold Medal awards in national competitions. In 1914, a travelling scholarship gave him the opportunity to visit several French cathedrals where he studied many magnificent stained glass pieces.

Clarke's first major commission was to design windows for the chapel for University College, Cork. His windows, completed in 1917, were received with critical acclaim. They established his reputation as an artist of exceptional originality and technical expertise, bringing a new dimension to modern stained glass. Clarke's stained glass windows, with their jewelled lights, deep rich colours and elaborate design, adorn many churches throughout Ireland. These include Castleknock Church, St Joseph's (Terenure), Newport, Co. Mayo, and Castlehaven, Co. Cork. The windows often afford startling contrasts to the dim interiors of the buildings.

Clarke also received many commissions from overseas. His masterpiece, 'The Geneva Window', was commissioned by the Irish government in 1927. Depicting scenes from the work of contemporary Irish writers, it is typical of his rich, glittering, diamond-like style. However, the work failed to receive government approval and in 1988, the Clarke family sold it to an American museum. Clarke was also a noted book illustrator, working on several classics such as Hans Christian Andersen's *Fairy Tales*, Edgar Allen Poe's *Tales of Mystery and Imagination*, Goethe's *Faust* and many others. Although he was not alone in achieving dual distinction as a stained glass artist and as an illustrator, Harry Clarke was exceptional in gaining an international reputation in both media.

Clarke taught design at the Metropolitan School of Art and was elected to the

Royal Hibernian Academy (RHA) in 1926. In 1930, he set up the Harry Clarke Studio at his home in 33 North Frederick Street. The last three years of his life were troubled with sickness. Despite travelling to Switzerland for rest and treatment, he died there in 1931, leaving a rich body of work despite his short life.

(1952-)

Eamonn Coghlan was born in Drimnagh, Dublin, on 21 November 1952. He was educated at the local Drimnagh Castle School and St Vincent's Christian Brothers School, Glasnevin. His running career kicked off with Celtic Athletic Club. With them, the young athlete learned the basic skills and disciplines in the nearby Phoenix Park. At the age of nineteen, Eamonn was offered an athletics scholarship to Villanova University in Pennsylvania. There he was coached by Jumbo Elliott, who had also worked with Ronnie Delany. Although he returned to Dublin after only six months, suffering from homesickness, he was persuaded to go back.

In 1973, Eamonn broke the Irish and European 1500 metres record in Jamaica. He represented Ireland the following year in the 5000 metres at the European Championships in Rome. Although he raced poorly, he was already marking his card for future success. He was now a member of Dublin's Donore Harriers which dominated Irish athletics during the 1970s and early 1980s. His final year at Villanova coincided with the 1976 Montreal Olympic Games. After winning his heat and semi-final in the 1500 m, Coghlan was considered a strong candidate in the final on 31 July. However, to his own frustration and the nation's disappointment, he finished fourth. Undaunted, he trained at 5000 m over the next four years in the Phoenix Park under Gerry Farnan who, despite heart surgery, continued coaching even from his bed.

By this time Eamonn had built up a huge American following. For ten years he had dominated the indoor circuit, becoming its highest money earner. A chain of Wanamaker Mile victories and other indoor successes in the US earned him the nickname, Chairman of the Boards.

Eamonn's ultimate goal was still Olympic Gold in Moscow 1980. However, just two weeks before the games, after a marvellously successful few days during which he won the 800 m and the 1500 m at the Europa Cup, he became ill. Tired and worried, he managed to qualify for the finals, but again finished fourth. In 1982 a painful achilles tendon injury forced him out of the lucrative indoor season. Determined to overcome this setback, Eamonn trained six hours daily before becoming the first man to crack the 3.50 Indoor Mile in February 1983.

Winning the 5000 m final at the Helsinki World Championships was the highlight of his career.

Off the track, Eamonn's achievements have been equally impressive. He has worked successfully for Bord Fáilte in promoting Irish tourism while running his own public relations and sports consultancy company. When he retired from racing in 1988, Eamonn, his wife and their four children decided to return to Dublin. In October 1990, he was appointed Chief Executive of BLE, the governing body of Irish athletics, although he retired in June the following year. He now concentrates his energies on track and field management in New York. In 1992 he became Marketing and Communications Executive for Our Lady's Hospital for Sick Children's Research Unit (Crumlin, Dublin).

Eamonn wins gold at Helsinki (above) and shows it off to Dublin's Lord Mayor Michael Keating (below)

EAMONN COGHLAN

(1890-1922)

Michael Collins was the youngest of eight children. He was born on 16 October 1890 near Sam's Cross, Clonakilty, Co. Cork. His father, a small farmer, was seventy-five years of age when Michael arrived. The youngster attended the local school where he was influenced by the teacher, Denis Lyons. Lyons was an old Fenian pledged to Ireland's independence from England who fostered a spirit of patriotism in his pupils. From there, Michael went to Clonakilty Secondary School and studied for the British postal service. In 1906 he went to London to work as a clerk in the post office before joining a firm of stockbrokers. In 1909, while still in London, Collins joined the Irish Republican Brotherhood (IRB). He had already been

elected secretary to the Gaelic League and the Gaelic Athletic Association (GAA). These two organisations, though they were meant to be non-political, became vehicles for political activity. Collins soon became treasurer in the IRB. He was convinced that Irish independence could only be achieved by physical force.

Returning to Ireland in January 1916, Collins's organisational talents were extremely valuable as preparations were made for rebellion. His financial skills were also developed in the accountancy firm of Craig Gardner. Collins spent much of his time at Volunteer training camps. During the Easter Rising of 1916, he served as a staff captain in the GPO in Dublin. Collins was lucky to escape execution. After the ceasefire he was imprisoned in Stafford (England) and at Frongoch (Wales) where his qualities as a magnetic leader emerged. On his release, he became very active in Sinn Féin. As director of the Volunteer movement, he drafted a new constitution which demonstrated his methodical approach. As he was also elected to the Supreme Council of the IRB, Collins was now an important figure in every major Republican group. Along with Cathal Brugha and Éamon de Valera, he emerged as one of the strongest Republican leaders in Ireland.

Following Sinn Féin's victory in the 1918 general election and the establishment of the first Dáil, Collins was appointed Minister of Home Affairs and later Minister for Finance. During this period he played a part in organising the daring escape of de Valera from Lincoln Prison. He also set up a system of Dáil loans which was very successful in raising money in the United States. During the War of Independence (1919–21), Collins organised the supply of weapons and developed an intelligence system to produce information about British military plans. He performed his many duties from several secret offices while on the run with a price on his head. Collins slept in 'safe' houses and often took great risks by cycling openly in the streets of Dublin. The British were worried by the success of Collins's underground network. They sent sixteen undercover agents to destroy him and his group. But Collins, however, became aware of the plan, and in November 1920, his own squad shot and killed eleven of the agents at various locations around Dublin. In a revenge attack later that day at Croke Park, fourteen spectators were killed and sixty wounded after a machine gun attack by the Black and Tans on the crowd and players. Two of Collins's men and an innocent bystander were also captured and tortured to death. Their deaths affected Collins deeply. By now, Collins was the most wanted man in Ireland. But the 'Big Fellow', as he was known, attended the funerals of his friends despite the presence of detectives and the army. In April 1921, Collins's family home in Co. Cork was burnt to the ground.

Following a truce with Britain on 11 July 1921, Collins was chosen as one of the Irish delegation that negotiated the Anglo-Irish Treaty which was finally signed on 6 December 1921. Collins had signed the agreement with great reluctance, considering it to be the best deal possible in the circumstances. Following a Dáil vote, the Treaty was ratified by a majority of seven votes. A new government was formed to administer the terms of the Treaty with Collins as chairman. A vicious civil war (1922–23) followed between the pro-Treaty Free State forces and the anti-Treaty group led by de Valera. Collins was now Commander-in-Chief of the pro-Treaty army.

On 22 August 1922, following a tour of inspection of pro-Treaty troops, Collins's convoy was ambushed at Beal na Bláth in Co. Cork. He was shot in the head and died almost immediately. Michael Collins died at the age of thirty-two and was buried in Glasnevin Cemetery, Dublin.

(521-597)

Colmcille, a name which means 'Dove of the Church', was born at Gartan, Co. Donegal, on 7 December 521. Of royal blood, he was a descendant of the High King, Niall of the Nine Hostages. Colmcille might have been a king himself, but instead he studied under Finian at Clonard, where he learned Latin, history and poetry. He studied at various monasteries including Moville, Co. Down, and Glasnevin, outside Dublin. After his ordination, he travelled around Ireland for many years, founding monasteries at Derry, Durrow (Laois), Swords (Dublin), Kells (Meath), Moone (Kildare) and Glencolmcille (Donegal). He is said to have performed many miracles, including turning spring water into altar wine at Moville.

The Battle of Cuildreimhne near Sligo, which was to make such an impact on Colmcille's life, took place in the year 561. The story is told that Colmcille borrowed a rare book from St Finian and secretly copied it out by hand—this was before the invention of the printing press. (Colmcille is said to have handwritten copies of 300 books during his lifetime.) Finian was furious. The two men asked Diarmuid, the High King of Ireland, to solve the case. Diarmuid's famous verdict was, 'To every cow her calf, to every book its copy.' Colmcille was annoyed with the decision so he called on his relations, the O'Neill's, to avenge him. Another story to explain the battle suggests that a hostage who took refuge with Colmcille was killed by Diarmuid. Whatever the cause, the Battle of Cuildreimhne ensued and 3,000 men were killed. Colmcille, horrified by the senseless slaughter, vowed to exile himself from Ireland. Another source claims he was ordered to convert as many pagans abroad as there were dead men on that battlefield.

In 563, with twelve companions, Colmcille sailed to Iona Island off the western coast of Scotland and established a monastery there. He then began his great mission of converting the Picts to Christianity. It was a busy life, building, farming, travelling, preaching and studying. Soon many other monasteries spread throughout Scotland.

One story tells how Brude, King of the Picts, who lived in a palace at Inverness, was visited by Colmcille. The King was flanked by magicians who tried to prevent Colmcille from entering the castle. But when the saint made the sign of the cross, the doors flew open. Later, the chief magician tried to drown out the Mass with loud noises, but Colmcille's voice rose above the thunder and the trumpet fanfare that the magicians created. King Brude was so impressed that he was converted to Christianity along with his people. Many other stories are told about Colmcille's journeys throughout Scotland, his miracles and his kindness to animals.

For all his missionary activity abroad, Colmcille had not forgotten his beloved Ireland. In 575, he returned to his native country to discuss the political position of the Scottish colony of Dál Riada (Argyll) with the High King, and obtained a promise of independence for the colony. Colmcille, a poet himself, also persuaded the King not to abolish the wandering poets, or *filidh*, who had recently been abusing their position. Instead, it was agreed that their activities should be controlled.

Colmcille's last years were spent on Iona. He was now leader of a large and growing Christian Church in Scotland. He died peacefully in June 597. His remains are believed to have been transferred to Downpatrick, Co. Down, to lie with those of St Patrick and St Brigid. Colmcille is one of Ireland's three patron saints. His feast day is on 9 June. Today, Iona attracts thousands of pilgrims who come to visit the place from which St Colmcille brought Christianity to northern Britain.

(1868-1916)

James Connolly was born in the Irish quarter of Cowgate, Edinburgh, on 5 June 1868. He was the third and youngest son of John and Mary Connolly who had emigrated from Ireland in the 1850s. Social conditions in Cowgate at the time were dreadful, with great poverty, overcrowding and disease.

James left school when he was eleven to work with his brother at the *Edinburgh Evening News* as a printer's 'devil'—the boy who cleaned the inky rollers. He went on to work in a bakery and then a tiling factory.

At fourteen, James falsified his age and enlisted in the British Army. Joining the Royals Scots Regiment, he was posted to the Curragh in Ireland. During this period James read avidly, developing his ideas about a better society. In Dublin he met Lillie Reynolds whom he married in 1890. When his battalion was ordered to Aldershot in 1891, Connolly deserted. He returned to Scotland where he became closely involved in the socialist movement and in the cause of Irish independence.

In 1892, Connolly took over as secretary of the Scottish Socialist Federation. He also became involved with the Independent Labour Party. Unsuccessful in the Scottish elections in April 1895, Connolly began to look for work as a political organiser outside Edinburgh. The Dublin Socialist Club invited him to become their organiser for a fee of £1.00 a week. In May 1896, Connolly sailed to Dublin, a city whose slums were worse than those in Edinburgh. There, he founded the Irish Socialist Republican Party. In 1897, with Maud Gonne, he demonstrated against the visit of Queen Victoria to Dublin and was arrested.

Connolly's writing skills were sharpened in countless articles and pamphlets on socialist issues, including 'Erin's Hope'. He was a fine speaker, lecturing in England and Scotland where he raised money to launch a weekly newspaper, *The Workers' Republic*, which was first published in August 1898. In 1902 and 1903, he visited the USA and spent the next seven years there. While in America, Connolly set up the Irish Socialist Federation in New York. He published a monthly magazine, *The Harp*, and founded the Industrial Workers of the World, whose aim was to organise all workers into one huge union.

In 1910, Connolly returned to Ireland and became Ulster organiser for the

Irish Transport Workers' Union. He was also asked to organise the new Socialist Party of Ireland. In 1913, dur-ing the employers' lock-out in Dublin, Connolly became the workers' leader following the arrest of James Larkin. Connolly himself was arrested and went on hunger strike, but was released after a week. Larkin and Connolly appealed for help from abroad and in September the first food ship sailed into Dublin.

Seeing that political action was needed, Connolly organised the Irish Citizen Army. When the Irish Republican Brotherhood (IRB) decided on armed rebellion in 1916, Connolly became mili-tary leader of the Citizen Army in Dublin.

During the Easter Rising of 1916, he led the GPO forces and was badly wounded when a bullet smashed his left ankle. One of the seven signatories of the Proclamation of the Irish Republic, Connolly was executed by a firing squad in Kilmainham Jail at dawn on 12 May 1916. His wounds were so severe that he was strapped to a chair for his execution.

A wounded James Connolly lies on a stretcher inside the GPO during the Rising of 1916

(1803-1878)

Paul Cullen was the third child in a family of sixteen. He was born near Prospect, Co. Kildare, on 29 April 1803. He received his early education at Shackleton Quaker School in Ballitore before entering Carlow College as a boarder in 1817.

In 1820, Cullen was offered a place at Maynooth College. But his father forbade him to do so because he did not want his son to take the oath of allegiance to the King of England. Instead, he entered the College of Propaganda in Rome which worked to extend the Church's teachings worldwide. He was ordained in 1829 and appointed Professor of Greek and Oriental Languages.

In 1832, Cullen was appointed Rector of the Irish College in Rome. Under his guidance, the college entered a period of great success, with numbers increasing every year. His experience in the college, where he had to deal with students from many nations, exposed him to different cultures and opinions. As the agent of the Irish bishops, he tried to counteract British influence in the Vatican. Meanwhile in Ireland, the bishops were split over the question of education. Most of them believed that the new system set up in 1831, in which the Church had no real control over schools, was the best they could hope for in the circumstances. The Irish bishops were prepared to give the new system a try. Cullen in general favoured the system but urged certain safeguards. Eventually, the bishops accepted Cullen's proposals.

During the terrible Famine years (1845–49), Cullen worked tirelessly organising relief. When Daniel O'Connell died in Genoa on 15 May 1847, Cullen played a leading part in arranging his funeral. In 1849, with Italy in the throes of revolution, Cullen became Rector of the College of Propaganda while still remaining Rector of the Irish College. Before long, the military powers in Italy ordered the Propaganda College to be taken over by the government. Cullen acted quickly, asking the US Minister for protection for American students in the college. When the American flag was flown over the building, the military take-over was abandoned.

In 1850, Cullen was consecrated as Archbishop of Armagh. He was also made Apostolic Delegate. Within three months of his return to Ireland, Cullen convened the

Synod of Thurles. It was the first Irish bishops' meeting in 700 years and its aim was to discuss the education controversy, poverty and other issues.

In 1852, Cullen was transferred to Dublin as Archbishop. In 1854, he helped set up a Catholic University under John Henry Newman, a brilliant English scholar who had converted from Anglicanism. Cullen campaigned vigorously against mixed education. The government, yielding to Cullen's demand for denominational liberty, set up the Powis Commission of Inquiry in 1869 which eventually recommended many of his proposals. Among them was his demand for the denominational training of teachers. In 1875 St Patrick's Training College, Drumcondra, was founded. On 1 Septem-ber 1859 Cullen opened the diocesan seminary, Holy Cross College, at Clonliffe. In 1861 he laid the founda-tion stone of the Mater Hospital. During this period he introduced many religious orders into the city.

Although Cullen had no sym-pathy for secret organisations, his plea for mercy saved Thomas F. Burke, the Fenian leader, from hanging. A strict disciplinar-ian, Cullen's busy schedule continued even as he grew old. In 1866, he became Ireland's first cardinal and took a leading part in the First Vatican Council. There, his definition of papal infallibility was adopted with minor modifications.

Cullen died on 24 October 1878. After a huge funeral, and according to his wishes, he was buried in the crypt at Clonliffe College.

St Peter's Rome, where Cardinal Cullen worked for many years. It was also the setting for the First Vatican Council

(1948-   )

Shaun Davey was born in Belfast on 18 January 1948 where he spent his early childhood before moving to Dublin while in his teens. On leaving school he began painting, but eventually entered Trinity College, Dublin. He left with a BA and a scholarship to London University where, for two further years, he took an MA at the Courtauld Institute of Fine Art.

When he returned to Dublin, Shaun lectured in the History of Art at NCAD (1975–77), and at TCD (1976–77). During this period he became a founding member of 'Bugle', an experimental band, with Donal Lunny. He also wrote music for TV and radio commercials. He made his début as a composer for theatre in 1976, with scores for 'Catchpenny Twist' and 'Kingdom Come'.

In 1979, Davey began 'The Brendan Voyage: Suite for Orchestra and Uilleann Pipes'. It is based on Tim Severin's voyage tracing St Brendan's reputed journey to the shores of America. As an album it has sold over 50,000 copies.

Further success followed including his first commission, 'The Pilgrim: Suite for Orchestra and Celtic Soloists' (1983), for the Lorient Interceltic Festival. 'Granuaile: Song Suite' (1985), based on the life of Grace O'Malley, received its USA première in New York in June 1991.

In 1985, Shaun Davey was a Rehab Person of the Year for his contribution to Irish culture. In 1986, he completed a concerto for uillean pipes and orchestra. He resumed his career in theatre music, writing the music for 'Fair Maid of the West' with the Royal Shakespeare Company (RSC). Since then, he has worked regularly with the RSC, the Mermaid and the Barbican Theatre, London. He has also composed music for theatre in Ireland: 'Peer Gynt' (1988), 'The Breadman' (1990), 'The Silver Tassie' (1990) and 'Prayers of Sherkin'.

In 1988 Davey received his second commission, a large-scale concert work for the city of Derry to commemorate the Siege of 1689. At the end of the première performance in Derry in May 1990, the audience responded with a five-minute standing ovation.

In 1990, Davey scored and recorded the music for the Granada TV programme

'Who Bombed Birmingham?' and BBC TV's 'Pentecost' by Stewart Parker. In September 1990, he accepted a commission from the Northern Irish Community Relations Council to compose a 'Double Harp Concerto' to be performed in 1992 at the Belfast Queens Festival commemorating the last great Irish festival of harping held in Belfast 200 years ago. His music for the RSC production of 'Troilus and Cressida' ran throughout the 1990–92 season.

SHAUN DAVEY

Detail from the 'Relief of Derry'
album cover

63

(1814-1845)

Thomas Davis was born in Mallow, Co. Cork, on 14 October 1814. His father, a British army surgeon, died just before Thomas's birth. In 1818, his mother moved to Dublin with her family to live in what is now 67 Baggot Street. This was to be Thomas's home for the rest of his life. At school, he was only an average student and had little interest in sport, although he tried to play handball and hurling for a while. When he was seventeen, he entered Trinity College, Dublin.

His four years at Trinity were an exciting experience for Davis. At this time, the college catered for both Catholic and Protestant students. Davis, a Protestant, found that this broadened his mind in many matters. Upon graduating in 1835, he

considered a career as a lawyer. However, he decided to travel abroad for a while before working, visiting England and the Continent. Returning three years later, he resumed his law studies in Trinity and became involved with the university's Historical Debating Society. In 1840 Davis, now President of the Society, spoke out in support of Irish independence and pleaded for Irish historical studies at Trinity.

At this time, Daniel O'Connell was attempting to repeal the Act of Union which allowed the parliament in London to rule Ireland. Impressed by O'Connell's political aims, Davis joined the National Repeal Association in 1839. Although he had great respect for the 'Liberator', Davis and O'Connell disagreed on many political issues. The most important dispute between them was about the methods employed to achieve independence. O'Connell maintained that there must be no bloodshed along the road to freedom, while Davis urged that fighting, although regrettable, was a necessary means to independence.

Davis soon became leader of a group of young men who were becoming increasingly frustrated with O'Connell's peaceful tactics. They were known as the Young Irelanders. In 1841, Davis and his two friends, John Blake Dillon and Charles Gavan Duffy, met in Dublin's Phoenix Park to discuss producing their own newspaper. Gavan Duffy agreed to finance the project. There and then, the hugely popular paper, *The Nation*, was born. The first issue appeared on 15 October 1842 and it soon built up a loyal readership of a quarter of a million people from all over Ireland. Unlike other papers of the time, *The Nation* provided much more than reports on the British parliament, military developments on the Continent and social gossip from Dublin. It gave Irish people an awareness of and pride in their own language, heritage and culture. The journal's slogan was 'Educate that you may be free.'

Poetry was published too, with Davis himself becoming the most regular contributor. Davis also wrote over fifty songs and many of his poems were set to music. Some, like 'A Nation Once Again' and 'The West's Asleep' remain popular to this day. Davis captured the imagination of the country with his belief in Irish freedom and was soon regarded as Ireland's national poet. In 1843, a collection of his best songs was included in *The Spirit of the Nation*.

Davis also intended to publish a series of cheap paperbacks about Ireland which he hoped poor people would buy. Some of the proposed books appeared and were enthusiastically received. But at the height of his success, when he was only thirty-one, Davis was taken ill in September 1845. He died a few days later (16th) of scarlet fever at his mother's house in Baggot Street. After a huge funeral, he was buried in Mount Jerome Cemetery. Davis's influence on the future course of Irish history was extremely important. His ideas lived on after him, laying a firm foundation for today's independent Irish republic.

THE NATION.

" To create and to foster public opinion in Ireland—to make it racy of the soil."—CHIEF BARON WOULFE.

DUBLIN, SATURDAY, OCTOBER 15, 1842.

THE NATION.

With all the nicknames that serve to delude and divide us—with all their Orangemen and Ribbonmen, Torymen and Whigmen, Ultras and Moderados, and Heaven knows what rubbish besides, there are, in truth, but two parties in Ireland : those who suffer from her National degradation, and those who profit by it. To a country like ours, all other distinctions are unimportant. This is the first article of our political creed; and as we desire to be known for what we are, we make it our earliest task to announce that the object of the writers of this journal is to organise the greater and better of those parties, and to strive, with all our soul and with all our strength, for the diffusion and establishment of its principles. This will be the beginning, middle, and end of our labours.

And we come to the task with a strong conviction that there never was a moment more favorable for such a purpose than the present. The old parties are broken, or breaking up, both in England and Ireland—Whiggery, which never had a soul, has now no body ; and the simplest partisan, or the most selfish expectant—who is generally a creature quite as unreasonable—cannot ask us to fix the hopes of our country on the fortunes of a party so weak and fallen. Far less can we expect anything from Toryism, which could only serve us by ceasing to *be* Toryism ; even in its new and modified form it means the identical reverse of all we require to make the masses in this country happier and better. But this shifting of parties—this loosening of belief in old distinctions and dogmas, has prepared men's minds for new and greater efforts. Out of the contempt for mere party politics will naturally grow a desire to throw aside small and temporary remedies—to refuse to listen any longer to those who would plaster a cut finger, or burn an old wart, and call this doctoring the body politic—and to combine for great and permanent changes. The point of honour which restrained multitudes from abandoning Whiggery, while their service could sustain it in its old accustomed place, can operate no more. The idiot hope, that Toryism might for once produce something good, has been pretty well disappointed ; and, after an unexampled lull in politics, the popular party are ready, and willing, and anxious once again to be up and doing.

Part of a page from an early edition of **The Nation**

THOMAS DAVIS

(1846-1906)

Michael Davitt was born in the village of Straide, Co. Mayo, on 25 March 1846. His father, a Catholic smallholder, was evicted after the dreadful potato famine which devastated Ireland at this time. In 1852, the family emigrated to Haslingden in Lancashire.

At eleven years of age, Michael was sent to work long hours every day in a cotton mill. His right arm had to be amputated after an accident there. Unable to work, he attended the local Wesleyan school. Davitt became involved in the Irish Republican movement and joined the Fenians in 1865. He took part in an unsuccessful attack on Chester Castle two years later. In 1868, he was made organising secretary of the Fenians in England and Scotland. In order to cover up his revolutionary activities, Davitt became a firearms salesman. However, his luck ran out in 1870 when he was sentenced to fifteen years in Dartmoor prison on a charge of treason. He was released after seven years, largely through the efforts of Isaac Butt, Charles Stewart Parnell and the Prison Amnesty Association.

Davitt then joined his family in America. There, he developed his plan to combine the movement for national independence with agitation for land reform. He was a keen advocate of land nationalisation but was prepared to accept peasant ownership as a lesser evil to landlordism. Returning to Ireland in 1878, this 'New Departure' was at first treated with suspicion by both the Republican movement and politicians such as Parnell. However, crop failures and falling farm prices meant that Davitt's plan was accepted by Parnell. In 1879, Davitt and Parnell founded the Irish National Land League. Parnell became its first president. The wide appeal of the Land League can be seen in the differing backgrounds of its founders—Davitt representing Catholic nationalism, whereas Parnell was a Protestant landlord.

The Land League undertook a long, bitter land war against unjust rents and evictions. Its membership included both constitutional and revolutionary nationalists and it was supported financially from America. During these land struggles, the ostracism of Captain Boycott, a landlord's agent in Mayo, added a new word to the English language to describe this tactic. In 1881, since the government felt pressurised by the League's popularity, it passed a Land Act which granted tenants the three F's—fair rent, fixed tenure and free sale. However, the League still had to continue its fight for the right of tenants to own the land.

Although the League leaders were arrested and the organisation was declared illegal by the British government, Davitt and Parnell joined forces again to set up the Irish National League. In 1885, the British government finally began to dismantle the landlord system. The partnership between Davitt and Parnell came to an end when Parnell became entangled in a famous divorce case.

In 1886 Davitt married an American, Mary Yore. His followers presented her with a house, Roselawn, in Ballybrack, Co. Dublin, which became known as the 'Land League Cottage'. Davitt represented parliament for the constituencies of Co. Meath, North Meath and South Mayo from 1882 to 1899. With the split in the Irish Party after the downfall of Parnell, Davitt's hopes for national independence were dashed. His final years, following his resignation from Westminster as a protest against the Boer War, were occupied with journalism. His books cover a wide range, from anti-Semitism in Russia (which he had visited many times) to convict life in Britain. These works include *Leaves from a Prison Diary* (1884), *The Boer Fight for Freedom* (1902) and *The Fall of Feudalism in Ireland* (1904). Davitt died of blood poisoning in Dublin on 31 May 1906 and was buried in his native Straide. A plaque

and a high cross mark the grave of Ireland's land reformer.

(1935-)

Ronald (Ronnie) Delany was born on 6 March 1935 in Arklow. His father was a customs and excise officer. The family moved to Dublin three years later. Ronnie received his early education at O'Connell's Primary School before attending Catholic University School, Leeson Street. By then, his natural athletic ability had brought him to the fore of schoolboy competitions, enabling him to receive a track scholarship to Villanova University, Pennsylvania, in 1954.

There he studied economics and marketing. He also trained hard at his running style and dominated American middle-distance running for the next eight years. His achievements on the indoor track were impressive. He won an amazing forty consecutive indoor races setting three consecutive world records for the indoor mile in the process. During the late 1950s, he was a hero in American athletics, where his popularity was boosted by intense media interest. Curiously enough, this aspect of his athletic career received scant attention in Ireland where indoor running had little following.

Early in 1956, Delany became the seventh man in history to run a sub four-minute mile in Compton, California. However, the Irish Olympic selectors were worried by his loss of form in the month leading up to the Melbourne Olympic Games that summer. But Delany was determined to represent Ireland in the 1500 m competition. He went back to his studies at Villanova and stepped up his training under coach, Jumbo Elliot. His determination won him a place in the squad and he managed to qualify for the 1500 metre final. Still, few thought he would take any of the medal positions. In tenth position at the bell, that acceleration which had won him so many indoor races in America suddenly powered him along the field as he picked off one runner after another. The crowd rose as Delany's green vest came flying off the last bend, with his high-stepping knee action and jerking shoulders. He broke the tape with his arms widespread in triumph before falling to his knees in prayer. He was nearly four metres ahead of the second runner, having covered the last lap in an amazing 54 seconds. Delany's winning time was a record for the event (3. 41.2). By now a national hero, he lowered his best mile record to 3.58.8 the following year and improved on this time yet again (3. 57.7) before a jubilant Dublin crowd in 1958. The same year he also won a European Championship bronze medal. During this period, he was undefeated in the US, winning 40 consecutive races, 33 of them over the mile. Further achievements included the fastest ever half-mile and mile double run on a single day and the World University Champion Title in 1961. Troubled by a constant achilles tendon injury, he retired from athletics. During this period he married Joan Riordan. The couple have four children.

Delany joined the Aer Lingus sales team while studying for a masters degree and worked in New York and San Francisco before returning to Dublin. In 1967 he joined B & I and later became assistant chief executive. In 1988 he left B & I after twenty-one years to start his own consultancy firm, Ronnie Delany and Associates, specialising in tourism, sports and leisure.

Delany has served with many organisations: Chairman of Cospoir, the National Sports Council; board member of the Health Education Bureau; Vice-president of the Royal National Lifeboat Institution; Director of the National Tourism Council, the Convention Bureau of Ireland and Dublin Tourism; An Gaisce, the President's Award Committee. He is currently the non-executive Chairman of the Council of the Credit Institutions' Ombudsman.

Ronnie Delany's homecoming in 1956 as Olympic 1,500 metres gold medallist

(1882-1975)

Éamon de Valera was born in Manhattan, New York, on 14 October 1882. When his Spanish father died in 1885, his Irish-born mother sent him to live with his grandmother in Bruree, Co. Limerick. After attending the local primary school he went to the Christian Brothers School at Charleville. The youngster had to walk seven miles to school and back every day.

When he was sixteen, de Valera won a scholarship to Blackrock College, Co. Dublin. In 1903, he became a professor of mathematics at Rockwell College, Co. Tipperary. He received a degree in mathematics from the Royal College and then returned to Dublin, teaching at Belvedere College, Carysfort Teacher Training College and at Maynooth.

Baptised Edward, he named himself Éamon when he became a member of the Gaelic League in 1908. Right throughout his long life, de Valera had a passionate interest in the Irish language and culture. It was through this interest in Irish that he met his wife, Sinéad, who taught him the language. De Valera was also an enthusiastic rugby footballer.

In 1913, de Valera joined the Irish Volunteers and was quickly promoted to captain of the Donnybrook company. Plans were being prepared for armed revolution and in 1915 he was sworn into the Irish Republican Brotherhood (IRB), a secret Republican society which aimed to overthrow British rule in Ireland. De Valera was involved in the landing of arms at Howth harbour from the *Asgard* in July 1914.

On Easter Monday, 24 April 1916, the Rising began in Dublin. De Valera and his men took over Boland's Bakery, using the tall building as a watchtower on the south-eastern routes to Dublin. After fierce fighting involving much death and destruction, the Irish rebels surrendered to the numerically superior British Army. Although de Valera was sentenced to death, his sentence was later commuted to life imprisonment.

After serving time in prisons at Dartmoor, Maidstone and Lewes, he was released in June 1917. Soon after he made a victorious entrance on to the political stage, easily winning a by-election in East Clare.

In October 1917, he was elected president of Sinn Féin, a party which was founded to achieve an independent Irish Republic. By this time, he had disassociated himself from the IRB. With World War I engulfing Europe, the British government tried to extend conscription to Ireland. Under de Valera, Sinn Féin opposed conscription. In May 1918, he was imprisoned once again, this time in Lincoln Jail. In an election the following December, Sinn Féin had a massive victory, gaining 73 seats (45 of their winning candidates, including de Valera, were prisoners). In January 1919, Dáil Éireann met for the first time in the Mansion House, Dublin. This assembly initiated the Government of the Irish Republic. De Valera escaped from Lincoln Jail, using a key smuggled inside a cake. Making his way back to Ireland, he was made President of the Dáil on 1 April 1919.

In May 1919, de Valera visited the United States in order to seek recognition for the Irish Republic and to raise a loan to finance the new country. He managed to raise six million dollars. He returned to find Ireland engaged in the bitter War of Independence. The Republican forces were forced to rely on guerrilla tactics against the larger better-equipped British Army. After months of ambushes, reprisals, burnings and killings, a truce was declared on 11 July 1921. The Anglo-Irish Treaty was signed on 6 December 1921. This agreement created an Irish state split by a border with its six northern counties remaining under British rule. De Valera himself was not a member of the negotiating team which had signed the Treaty. Upon learning of the terms, he declared that he would not support its

acceptance. Following a sharp debate in the Dáil which broke many friendships within Sinn Féin, the Treaty was endorsed in January 1922, with 64 delegates in favour and 57 opposed. Arthur Griffith replaced de Valera as President and a Provisional Government of the new Irish Free State was elected.

The split between the pro-treaty and anti-treaty groups widened. When the army of the Provisional Government opened fire on the anti-treaty Republicans who had taken over the Four Courts in Dublin, the country was torn by a year of brutal civil war. Old comrades who had fought together in the War of Independence now turned against each other. Almost 800 people died before the Civil War ended in May 1923.

In April 1926, de Valera formed a new party, Fianna Fáil (Soldiers of Destiny). It won 44 out of 155 seats in the 1927 election. Up to then, the anti-treaty members of the Dáil had refused to take the oath of allegiance to the British monarch. However, the political cost of this refusal was high as it meant they were barred from entering the Dáil. De Valera and his followers eventually decided to sign. They declared it to be an empty formula because they had not spoken the words of the oath.

In 1931, de Valera's dream of a Republican paper was realised with the appearance of the *Irish Press* which was a major support to Fianna Fáil. They won 72 seats in the 1932 election and de Valera became head of the first Fianna

Fáil government. One of his first decisions while in power was to abolish the oath of allegiance. He also halted the payment of land taxes to Britain. These measures resulted in harsh British sanctions, with Ireland's agricultural community suffering the effects of this economic war.

A new Constitution followed in 1937 reflecting de Valera's Catholic Republican viewpoint. The state was renamed Eire or Ireland, with de Valera as Taoiseach (Prime Minister). In 1938, the economic war with Britain ended with the signing of the Anglo-Irish Agreement.

At this stage, de Valera was also making an international impact. As Minister for External Affairs, he was President of the Council of the League of Nations. In an impressive speech, he asked that all member countries respect the rules of the League. De Valera won admiration for his work at the League of Nations, where he supported disarmament and the settling of disputes by peaceful means.

During World War II, de Valera stood up to pressure from the main powers who wanted him to end Ireland's neutral position. In 1941 he successfully protested against a proposal to extend British conscription to Northern Ireland. During that year, he ordered fire engines to Belfast when the city was bombed by German aircraft.

In the mid 1930s he had declared the IRA to be an illegal organisation. During the war, its members were imprisoned, a few were executed and three died on hunger strike.

In 1948, the first Coalition Government removed Fianna Fáil after sixteen years in power. However, de Valera was back in government again in 1951. Plagued by continual eye problems since the 1920s, he was by then left with limited eyesight and unable to read. After another short interval of Coalition Government (1954–57) de Valera, now seventy-five years of age, won the general election of 1957. In June 1959, although his proposal to substitute direct voting for proportional representation was defeated, he was elected to the presidency of Ireland. He was re-elected in 1966 for a second term of seven years at the age of eighty-three. He retired from office in 1973 and died in Dublin two years later on 29 August 1975 at the age of ninety-two.

Éamon de Valera on his 91st birthday

(1889-1980)

Frank Duff was born on 7 June 1889 at 55 St Patrick's Road, Drumcondra, Dublin. His education began in the Little Dame School run by laywomen. From there he went to Belvedere before enrolling in Blackrock College where he became friendly with Éamon de Valera. He was well known as a practical joker and this mischievous humour stayed with him through life.

Duff was quite clever at school, but since his father had to retire early due to ill health, he decided against university study. At the age of nineteen he entered the civil service in order to help support the family. His career began in the Land Commission. He later worked at the Department of Agriculture and the Department of Finance.

Concerned at the plight of Dublin's poor, Duff joined the Society of St Vincent de Paul in 1914. This was a turning point in his life. It brought him into close contact with social problems such as unemployment, overcrowding, homelessness, disease, prostitution and crime. With his friend, Matt Lalor, a social worker, Duff founded the Legion of Mary in 1921. The first enrolments took place at Myra House, Francis Street, Dublin. There was some initial opposition to the Legion of Mary. The Archbishop of Dublin viewed this lay organisation with such suspicion that he did not give approval to the official Legion handbook until 1953. The Jesuits were also slow to support Duff's organisation. Yet the Legion went from strength to strength and devoted itself to voluntary apostolic and social work, chiefly among the poorer sections of the population. The movement eventually expanded from its base in Dublin to Waterford before taking root in Scotland. It soon spread abroad to Australia, Africa, America and Asia. Legion work all over the world included visiting hospitals, prisons and sick people in their homes, as well as working with youth groups, caring for destitute men and women and assisting alcoholics and prostitutes.

The Legion promoted devotion to the Virgin Mary. Duff himself wrote a number of works on Marian theology, including *The Legion of Mary Handbook, The Spirit of the Legion of Mary, Walking with Mary* and *Mary Shall Reign*. He also gave religious instructions to children after Sunday Mass.

In 1928, Duff founded the Morning Star hostel in Dublin, a shelter for homeless men. In 1931, the Legion set up the Sancta Maria hostel which catered for the reform of prostitutes and the care of unmarried mothers and their children.

Following his retirement from the Civil Service in 1933, Duff transferred his energies to organising the Legion at its headquarters at De Montfort House. During World War II, Praesidia (Legion branches) were formed in army units, in prison camps and among the suffering populations of occupied countries. Duff attended the Second Vatican Council in 1963 as an observer, but he was wary of new developments in the Church and was worried by those whose views downgraded the status of the Virgin Mary. Granted the Papal Order of St Gregory the Great, he was received and commended by Pope Paul VI. He was granted an honorary LL.D. from the National University of Ireland in recognition of his unstinting work on behalf of the poor.

Frank Duff's lifetime of service to the underprivileged continued right up to the end of his life. Although ninety-one, he had been cycling around the city, as was his habit, up to a short time before his death in the Morning Star hostel on 7 November 1980.

FRANK DUFF

(1767-1849)

Maria Edgeworth was born at Black Bourton, Oxfordshire, on 1 January 1767. She was the second child of her father's first marriage. Richard Lovell Edgeworth was to marry three more times after the death of Maria's mother. He was both a progressive landlord and an inventor. Maria spent most of her childhood in England before travelling to her father's estate in Edgeworthstown (Mostrim), Co. Longford, in 1782. She remained there for the rest of her long life, with the exception of occasional visits to London and the Continent.

Maria soon took over the reins of responsibility on her father's estate, a job which gave her a wide knowledge of Irish life. She was also governess to the twenty-two children of her father's four marriages. She wrote in the living room, a marvellous feat of concentration with all the bustle of family life around her. Her first published work, *Letters for Literary Ladies* (1795), owed much to her father's views on the education of women. *The Parent's Assistant*, a collection of children's stories, followed in 1796. She collaborated with her father on *Practical Education* (1798). Maria was influenced greatly by her father. He supervised her work, managed her literary career and for nearly half a century he frequently edited her work.

Maria's first novel, *Castle Rackrent* (1800), was a great success. The book narrated the history of a severe landlord and his family, the Rackrents. It has been described as the first regional novel in the English language. Although published anonymously at first, Maria's name appeared on subsequent editions of the book. It had a major influence on the regional novels of the writer, Sir Walter Scott, whom she visited in 1832. They became firm friends, with Scott returning her visit two years later at Edgeworthstown.

Maria's letters present a vivid picture of Irish life in her day. Free and frank, they were not subject to her father's scrutiny. A second novel, *Belinda*, followed in 1801. She again joined forces with her father in *Essays on Irish Bulls* (1802), a humorous collection. In the same year she travelled to Brussels and Paris. Regretfully turning down a proposal of marriage from a Swedish nobleman because of her family responsibilities, she returned to Edgeworthstown in 1803. There she continued her lifestyle of writing, estate management and governess. *Leonora*, a novel, was published in 1806. *Tales of Fashionable Life*, published in six volumes (1809–1812), was a financial success for Maria. *The Absentee* (1809) and *Ormond* (1817) were based on her shrewd observation of Irish life. The former looked angrily at the social damage caused by absentee landlords. During a visit to London in 1813, Maria met many great literary personalities of the time. Byron, Austen, Macauley, Thackeray and Turgenev all admired her work.

After her father's death in 1817, Maria's literary output slowed down. Her energy was increasingly sapped in managing the estate. Eye trouble also forced her to cut back on her writing. However, she did publish another novel, *Helen*, in 1834, and completed her father's memoirs. As manager of the Edgeworth estate, Maria did much to ease the suffering of her tenants during the Famine. She died on 22 May 1849 at Edgeworthstown, in the arms of Frances Edgeworth, her stepmother and closest friend.

Edgeworthstown House, the home of Maria Edgeworth

(1778-1803)

Robert Emmet was born at St Stephen's Green West on 4 March 1778. His father, Dr Robert Emmet, was doctor to the Lord Lieutenant of Ireland. His brother was Thomas Addis Emmet of the United Irishmen. An intelligent pupil, Emmet received his early education at private schools before entering Trinity College at the age of fifteen.

Emmet quickly built up a reputation as a fine speaker, becoming an impressive debater in Trinity's Historical Society. No doubt influenced by his brother's revolutionary convictions, he became a member of the United Irishmen while at college. In April 1798, the Lord Chancellor visited Trinity to assess the strength of support for the United Irishmen and expelled a group of revolutionary students. As a gesture of support against this, Emmet struck his name off the college register. By so doing, he destroyed any hope he had of a professional career. With a warrant out for his arrest, he left Ireland. His brother Thomas had been deported to Scotland after the 1789 Rebellion and was banned from ever returning. Emmet joined his brother and discussed the possibility of another rising with him.

In 1802, he sailed for France in an effort to persuade the French to help the cause of Irish independence. Emmet hoped that the French, bitter rivals of the English, might supply soldiers and arms. However, Napoleon, the French ruler, did not provide immediate assistance. A frustrated Emmet, his patience worn thin by delays and half-promises, returned home in October 1802. Yet he was still determined to organise a rebellion. He was still a wanted man and often had to disguise himself and travel under false names to avoid capture.

Throughout the winter of 1802, Emmet laid plans. He gathered volunteers for his cause, secretly trained men, bought arms and arranged safe houses for supplies. He also tested an explosive rocket at Rathfarnham. He arranged for Thomas Russell, a friend of Wolfe Tone, to lead the rising in Ulster.

Meanwhile in Europe, France and England were at war again. Emmet hoped to begin the rebellion at the same time as Napoleon's expected invasion of England. But due to an accidental explosion in one of his weapon stores, Emmet's rebellion was brought forward. He was afraid the British would investigate and thought it better to act while he had surprise on his side.

On 23 July 1803 Emmet, dressed in a green uniform and cocked hat, set out to capture Dublin Castle which held the British forces' gun supply. Some of his men, however, failed to turn up and many others were untrained. So Emmet's army was weak. They killed the Lord Chief Justice, Lord Kilwarden, a popular man who happened to be riding by in his carriage at the time. In the attack Kilwarden's nephew was also killed.

These incidents lost Emmet's rebellion much public support. Before long, his army was scattered. Emmet himself escaped to the Dublin mountains. Thomas Russell's rising in Ulster did not even begin. A full-scale British operation under Major Sirr and Major Swann began to round up the rebels. Night-time arrests became common. Even Emmet's mother and his loyal housemaid, Anne Devlin, were imprisoned. Although Emmet could have escaped to France, his love for Sarah Curran, to whom he was secretly engaged, kept him in Dublin despite all dangers. Eventually, in a house at Harold's Cross near Dublin, Emmet was arrested by Major Sirr after being betrayed by an informer.

A trial followed which is remembered above all for Emmet's famous speech from the dock which finished: 'When my nation takes her place among the nations of the earth, then, and not till then, let my epitaph be written.' He was sentenced to death for plotting to overthrow the government. Even though his rebellion was a failure, he believed that when Ireland eventually gained its freedom, his actions might be understood.

On 20 September 1803, at the age of twenty-five, Robert Emmet was hanged in front of St Catherine's Church in Thomas Street, Dublin, before a large crowd.

(1782-1837)

John Field was born on 26 July 1782 in Golden Lane, near South Circular Road, Dublin. He was the eldest son of Robert Field, a violinist at the Theatre Royal, Crow Street. His father and his grandfather carried on a small music school to supplement the family income. They gave Field his early passion for music. When the youngster showed signs of musical promise, he was regarded as a potential asset to the family purse. At nine years of age he was considered such a remarkable prodigy on the piano that he was sent for a course of finishing lessons with Giordani, a leading figure in Dublin's musical life. Master Field made his first official début on 24 March 1792, playing at three concerts in the Rotunda Assembly Rooms, Dublin.

Newspaper reviews commented on the astonishing performance by such a young child.

Robert Field believed that his son was destined to become a great musician. In 1793, the family left Ireland for Bath in England, and eventually moved to London. The father took a part in the Haymarket Theatre orchestra. John was sent to Muzio Clementi, the most important piano teacher of the day, paying a fee of 100 guineas. Clementi became the main influence on the boy for the next ten years. The highlight of John's first year in London was a visit by Haydn. The famous composer heard Field play in 1794 and his praise must have given immense encouragement to the young virtuoso.

The first authentic specimen of Field's own composition—a single page of thirty-one bars—is dated 1796. In February 1799, Field won his first success as a composer when his Piano Concerto in E Flat was heard. It was performed with his proud father playing violin in the orchestra while Clementi watched appreciatively. Field had already embarked on a teaching career when, in 1802, Clementi brought him to Paris. Clementi felt that a wider experience of life and music would benefit his young charge. John's performance of Bach and Handel fugues from memory astonished French musicians. After spending some time in Vienna, they journeyed to St Petersburg. Field's success there whetted his appetite for further recognition and he travelled to other cities including Riga and Moscow, which became his favourite base for many years. His marriage to a Frenchwoman in 1810 was not a particularly happy one.

Field never neglected his technical practice, constantly striving for greater perfection. His fame spread beyond Russia over the next three decades and he gave successful concerts throughout Europe. He taught piano for high fees. Among his pupils was the Russian musician, Glinka.

With his health deteriorating, Field decided to return to London after an absence of thirty years. He wanted to see his aged mother who was now a widow. In 1832, although his E Flat Piano Concerto was warmly received in London, tastes had changed in Europe. Field was no longer the centre of attention and Chopin was the new star on the musical horizon. Field's mother died in July that same year. Despite a serious illness which caused him much pain, he continued to perform on a European tour from 1832 to 1833. Hospitalised in Naples for a year, he was brought back to Moscow by a wealthy Russian family, the Romanoffs.

Field died on 11 January 1837 as a result of pneumonia following a chill received during the cold Moscow winter of 1836–37. He was buried in Wedensky Cemetery outside Moscow. For years his memory was kept green in Russia whilst it had faded elsewhere. Besides the brilliance and expressiveness of his playing, he is famous as the inventor of the nocturne, a slow piano piece. He wrote about twenty nocturnes as well as seven concertos and four sonatas. The recital room in Dublin's National Concert Hall was recently named in his honour.

JOHN FIELD

(1926-)

Garret FitzGerald was born in Dublin on 9 February 1926. His parents were both prominent in the struggle for Irish independence and in the foundation of the new state. When he was two, the family moved from Donnybrook to Bray, Co. Wicklow, where he attended St Brigid's primary school. Completing his primary education in the Irish-speaking Coláiste na Rinne (Ring College), Co. Waterford, he then attended the Jesuit secondary school, Belvedere College, Dublin. In 1946 he graduated from University College, Dublin, in History, French and Spanish. Although called to the bar he did not practise as a barrister.

A year after leaving university FitzGerald joined Aer Lingus, the Irish national airline. From 1951 to 1958, as Research and Schedules Manager, he was in charge of scheduling charters, fares and costing the purchase of new aircraft. These duties demonstrated an amazing facility with timetables and statistics. His writings on economic aspects of air transport were widely published.

Leaving Aer Lingus in 1958, his economic expertise resulted in his becoming Dublin correspondent of the *Financial Times*. He was later Managing Director of the *Economist* Intelligence Unit of Ireland. His journalistic career has been a lengthy one. At various periods he has worked for papers in Britain, America, Canada, South Africa, Kenya, India, Australia, New Zealand and Hong Kong. He was also economic columnist of *The Irish Times* for almost twenty years, and resumed this column in September 1991.

Dr FitzGerald lectured in economics at University College, Dublin, from 1956 to 1973, concentrating on European Communities affairs and on transport economics. In 1958–59, he was Rockefeller Research Assistant in Trinity College, Dublin. His political career began in 1965 when he was elected to the Senate. Four years later, he was elected to the Dáil. He has been a Fine Gael TD for Dublin South East from 1969 to date. Rising rapidly within the party, he was Minister for Foreign Affairs from 1973 to 1977, a portfolio which gave his interest in European issues political thrust. Leading up to Ireland's membership of the EC, he was a major promoter of Irish entry through articles and lectures. Within weeks of Ireland joining the

EC in 1972, he became a member of the Council of Ministers of the EC. While there, he worked to develop Ireland's role. FitzGerald's other chief political concern was Northern Ireland. As Minister for Foreign Affairs, he broke new ground by regularly visiting the North, meeting a wide cross-section of political and cultural figures there. He was a major participant in negotiating the Sunningdale Agreement (December 1973) which led to a power-sharing Executive of Nationalists and Unionists. It was, however, later brought down by a political strike in 1974. Under this agreement it was decided that no change in the status of Northern Ireland could be made without permission of the majority of the population there—a stance he had been advocating for some time.

Dr FitzGerald was responsible for organising Ireland's first presidency of the EC in 1975 which was seen as a most successful one. He was also involved in the Lomé Agreement between the EC and forty-six African, Caribbean, Indian Ocean and Pacific countries (ACP). He also worked to steer Portugal into democracy. In 1976 he represented the EC in treaties signed with Tunisia, Algeria and Morocco.

Following the resignation of Liam Cosgrave in 1977, FitzGerald became leader of Fine Gael and set about restructuring the party after a nationwide tour. From June 1981 to March 1982, and again from December 1982 to March 1987, he was Taoiseach, leading coalition governments with the Labour Party. His Constitutional Crusade, launched in 1981 in an effort to create a more pluralist society in Ireland, floundered on the reefs of political and economic difficulties. In 1984, as President of the European Council, he developed plans for Portugal's eventual membership of the EC.

In 1983, as Taoiseach, he took part in the New Ireland Forum. Although Irish constitutional Nationalist parties attended, Unionists declined to participate. The Forum drew up guidelines for the resolution of the Northern Ireland problem and proposed models for eventual Irish unity. In November 1985, FitzGerald signed the Anglo-Irish Agreement on Northern Ireland with the British Prime Minister. An Inter-governmental Council, co-chaired by the Irish Minister for Foreign Affairs and the British Secretary of State, with a base in Belfast, was established. This gave the Irish government direct involvement in decisions concerning Northern Ireland. He was also involved in the International Fund which tried to undo the effects of the violence in the North.

In 1987, Dr FitzGerald resigned the leadership of Fine Gael and returned to the party back benches. He is now a director of Guinness Peat Aviation, the world's leading aircraft leasing company; of Comer International; of the Trade Development Institute which provides marketing help to many Third World countries; and also of the Corporate Finance Group. He has continued his journalistic work and lectures widely on European affairs, Anglo-Irish relations and political philosophy.

In 1991, his autobiography, *All in a Life*, was published. Other publications include: *State Sponsored Bodies* (1959); *Planning in Ireland* (1969); *Towards a New Ireland* (1972); *Unequal Partners* (1979) and *The Israeli/Palestinian Issue* (1990). He has been awarded honorary degrees by many universities including New York, St Louis, St Mary's Halifax (Canada), Keele (England), Boston (Massachusetts), Oxford (England) and the National University of Ireland. Other awards include the Grand Cross Order of Merit (Germany), Grand Cordon of the Order of the Rising Sun (Japan) and Order of Christ (Portugal).

Garret FitzGerald talking with British Prime

nister Margaret Thatcher

(1854-1920)

William Percy French was born on 1 May 1854 at the family residence, Cloonyquin House, Co. Roscommon. His father, Christopher, was a Doctor of Law and Justice of the Peace. His mother was the daughter of a Protestant rector. During his childhood, French developed a love of the countryside and its people. Musical evenings spent at Cloonyquin or in neighbours' houses revealed a talent for music and improvisation, especially on the banjo.

French first went to preparatory school in Derbyshire, then to Windermere College and later to Foyle College. Entering Trinity College, he took a civil engineering degree in 1881. He enjoyed life at Trinity, playing lawn tennis and painting watercolours as well as studying. For a college concert in 1877, he wrote the ballad 'Abdulla Bulbul Ameer'. The song became very popular, but was pirated by a London publisher who printed a slightly changed version without mentioning French's name.

French joined the Board of Works as surveyor of drains in Co. Cavan. This became his home for seven years and inspired the well-known song, 'The Effusion of William, Inspector of Drains'. He found time to paint the landscape and his delicate watercolours took several prizes at Dublin exhibitions. His song 'Phil the Fluther's Ball' was based on a small farmer from Leitrim who held dances in his little house in order to raise money for rent. Another song, 'Come back Paddy Reilly to Ballyjamesduff', was published in 1912. It was written in memory of an acquaintance who had emigrated to America.

Having learned from his early problem with 'Abdulla', French had his songs published by Pigotts, the reputable Dublin firm. In 1889 'Shlathery's Mounted Fut', describing the adventures of a Volunteer force, was published with great success. In 1890 he married Ettie Armitage-Moore, daughter of an estate agent, despite opposition from her family.

By January 1889, the Cavan drainage scheme was completed and Percy accepted the post of editor to a comic magazine called *The Jarvey*. Early in 1891, he began his collaboration with the Dublin musician, Collisson, a partnership that lasted thirty years. Together they wrote an Irish musical comedy, the first of its type, *The Knight of the Road*. French wrote the lyrics and

Collisson the music. It played to packed houses in the Queen's Theatre. French also wrote articles and gave painting lessons. Tragedy struck, however, when Ettie died in childbirth. The baby survived for only a few weeks.

French had lost most of his savings by investing in a distillery that was not successful. To support himself, he put on a series of variety shows which became very popular all over the country. In 1892 his opera, *Strongbow*, although not a success, introduced him to Helen Sheldon whom he married in 1894. The previous year he had produced a musical comedy, *Midsummer Madness*, which was warmly received. French now began touring in earnest. One day he arrived late for a concert in Kilkee, Co. Clare, because of delays on the West Clare Railway. This led him to write his popular 'Are ye right there, Michael?' which pokes fun at the railroad.

One summer's day, while resting on the cliffs of Skerries near Dublin, the sight of the Mourne Mountains in the distance inspired French's famous song, 'The Mountains of Mourne'. In 1910, with Collisson, he toured America, Canada, Bermuda, the West Indies and Panama. During World War I he travelled with his musical partner to entertain the troops. His later songs, 'Jim Wheelahan's Automobeel' (1903), 'Maguire's Motor Bike' (1906) and 'Flanagan's Flying Machine' (1911) reflected the influence of new inventions which were changing the world.

Early in 1920, while travelling home from Glasgow, French was taken ill. He died a week later of heart failure on 24 January at the age of sixty-five. He was buried in the Protestant churchyard at Formby, Lancashire.

Kilkee railway station on the West Clare line

(1929-)

Brian Friel was born in Killyclogher, near Omagh, Co. Tyrone, on 9 January 1929. His father, Patrick Friel, was the local headmaster and his mother was a post-mistress. Friel received his early education at the primary school in Culmore where his father was the principal. When his family moved to Derry, Friel went to Long Tower School and completed his secondary education at St Columb's College, Derry. From there, in 1945, he went to St Patrick's College, Maynooth. Instead of the priesthood, however, he took a post-graduate course in St Joseph's Training College, Belfast, before qualifying as a teacher in 1950.

For the next decade, following in the footsteps of his father, he taught in various schools in Derry. It was during this period

that his writing career began to develop. Many of his short stories appeared in the *New Yorker* magazine. He also wrote radio plays for the BBC. Although a full-time teacher and a family man with five children (he married Anne Morrison in 1954), his commitment to writing was total. In 1959 his first stage play, *A Doubtful Paradise*, was performed in Belfast.

In 1960, Friel retired from teaching to work full time as a writer. In 1962, many of the short stories already published were collected in *The Saucer of Larks*. It was as a playwright, however, that Friel's genius found its medium. In 1963, the Abbey Theatre staged *The Enemy Within*, and for the next two decades premièred most of Friel's plays.

Friel's first major theatrical success was *Philadelphia, Here I Come* (1964). It was a stunning work of style and artistic authority, as well as being the success of that year's Dublin Theatre Festival. This play was built around the theme of emigration. It used two actors to portray different sides of the main character's personality. In 1966, the play was produced on Broadway. Friel's second collection of short stories, *The Gold in the Sea*, was published in England and America during the same year. Further success followed with the Broadway première of *The Loves of Cass Maguire* (1967).

His artistic output climaxed with *Faith Healers* (1980), *Aristocrats* and *Translations* (1981), all appearing in a fertile 18-month period. *Translations*, one of Friel's most admired works, was the first production of the Field Day Theatre

Company and publishing house which was founded by Friel and the actor, Stephen Rea. Field Day has produced most of Friel's plays since *Translations*, including his version of Chekhov's *Three Sisters* (1981), *The Communication Cord* (1983) and *Making History* (1988).

Friel's latest play, *Dancing at Lughnasa* (1990), deals with themes of loyalty and disintegration within a family. It was staged at the Abbey Theatre, Dublin and the National Theatre, London. *Lughnasa* was a phenomenal success. It received the Olivier Award, further strengthening Friel's reputation as Ireland's premier living playwright. In October 1991, the play transferred to Broadway, receiving huge acclaim. In 1992, it received theatre's supreme accolade, winning three Tony awards. Later in the year, *Dancing at Lughnasa* returned to the Abbey Threatre. Now living across the border in Greencastle, near Moville, his involvement with the Field Day Theatre Company and his publishing base have been intense since 1980.

Among honours bestowed upon Friel was his election to the Irish Academy of Letters (1972), membership of Aosdana (1982), and an honorary Doctor of Literature from the National University of Ireland (1982). In 1987, he became the first Irish writer since W. B. Yeats to be nominated to a seat in the Irish Senate.

In 1989, BBC Radio devoted a six-play season to the works of Brian Friel. This was an unprecedented but deserved acknowledgment of Ireland's most important living playwright. In 1991, the Glenties Summer School devoted its entire programme to a celebration of Friel's work. Friel's newest work, *London Vertigo* (January 1992), is based on a play by the eighteenth-century Irish actor, Charles Macklin.

Dearbhla Molloy in* Dancing at Lughnasa *at the Abbey Theatre

(1939-   )

James Galway was born in Belfast on 8 December 1939. His father was a riveter in the Harland and Wolff shipyards, and his mother worked as a winder in a spinning mill. Both parents were musical. His mother played the piano while his father was a talented flute player. Galway began his own musical career with a mouth organ and a tin whistle before progressing to the flute.

James Galway was a lively boy, often getting into trouble with his mischievous pranks. One day, his middle finger was shattered while playing with a bullet. For weeks he could only play the flute using the little finger instead of the third. At nine years of age, he became a member of the Onward Flute Band, of which his uncle was band-master and conductor. Galway then went to his father's friend, Ardwell Dunning, to study music. He became so absorbed in music that his work at Mountcollyer Secondary School

suffered. By this time he had joined the Belfast Military Band. It was not until he entered the Irish Flute Championship that those around him began to recognise his real potential. Galway surprised everyone by boldly entering all three classes in the solo section (10–13 year old, 13–16 and the open class). He won all three.

On leaving school, Galway was apprenticed to a piano firm from Belfast for 23 shillings a week. At this stage, he was playing with Belfast's Youth Orchestra, with the 39th Old Boys Band, and with a small semi-amateur group called the Studio Orchestra. At fourteen, he was offered an audition at the Royal College of Music in London. The Belfast Education Committee awarded him a grant. He stayed with John Francis who taught flute at the college, living in his home as one of the family for three years.

As part of his audition for the Royal College, Galway was tested in sight reading. Although he had turned up without his glasses, he was able to play the piece from memory. In 1959, he moved to the famous Guildhall School of Music and Drama in London under the guidance of Geoffrey Gilbert.

In 1960, Galway received a grant enabling him to attend the renowned Paris Conservatoire. There, the competitive international atmosphere and his study under respected woodwind professors gave his playing an extra edge. He also earned money by busking on the Metro.

Galway then joined the Sadler's Wells Opera (1961–66) where Colin Davis was musical director. In 1965, he also played with the Covent Garden Opera orchestra. Before long, he signed a contract with the London Symphony Orchestra (1966–67) as first flute, touring abroad with them on many occasions. He married a French girl, Claire Le Bastard, but they were later to divorce.

Galway joined the BBC symphony Orchestra as flautist and piccolo player and also played with the Royal Philharmonic Orchestra (1967–69). He made a major career decision by joining Berlin's great orchestra as principal soloist under its conductor, Herbert von Karajan. From 1969 to 1975, they travelled all over the world.

However, James Galway wanted to pursue a career as a soloist. Despite opposition from von Karajan, he left the orchestra in July 1975. With his second wife and their children, he moved to Lucerne. Within the next two years, he made six solo recordings, toured more than twenty countries and appeared on countless TV shows. James Galway, the Irishman with the Golden Flute, was now internationally renowned, both as a performer and also for his master classes arising from his position as professor at the Eastman School of Music in Rochester in New York State.

Galway's flute sound is unique, producing a tone that moves from silver delicacy to heavy richness. He has adapted many concertos originally written for other instruments for the flute. He now appears before huge audiences and is a top-selling recording artist. His phenomenal popularity is testimony to his bubbling personality and impish sense of humour, as well as his outstanding musical ability. His life story, *An Autobiography*, was published in 1978. Other publications include *Flute* (1982) and *James Galway's Music in Time* (1983).

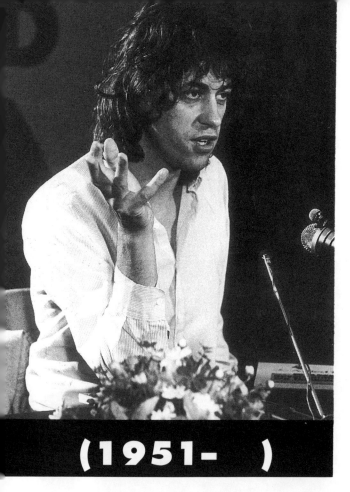

(1951-   )

Robert Frederick Geldof was born on 5 October 1951 in Blackrock, Co. Dublin. The family was very close, although his father, a travelling salesman, only came home at weekends. This happiness was not to last, however. The family moved to a gloomy house in Dun Laoghaire just before Bob began school. Soon after, tragedy struck when Bob's mother died from a brain haemorrhage. His sister, Cleo, looked after the family until she got married. When his other sister, Lynn, also left, Bob spent much time alone. During this period Bob suffered from asthma. He became troublesome at school in Blackrock College and was punished both at school and by his father who was disappointed with his progress. This made Bob feel unwanted and so he rebelled even more. However, Bob's behaviour masked a sensitivity to the misfortunes of others. He joined the Simon Community, a Christian organisation which helped the homeless and down-and-outs. This, of course, left him less time for schoolwork. As a result, he was the only one of his class in 1969 to fail his Leaving Certificate examination.

After a few part-time jobs, Bob moved to a squat in London in 1971. Following a police raid, Bob and his fellow squatters were charged with possessing cannabis. Although found not guilty, Bob decided to leave London to make a fresh start.

After teaching English in Spain, he returned to Dublin before moving to Canada where he became music editor of a paper. He returned again to Dublin, determined to set up his own magazine, but found no financial backing for the project. At this time some of his old pals had started their own pop group, the Nightlife Thugs. Bob was made lead singer because his efforts on the tambourine were so bad. He also became the group's manager and spokesman. In 1975 they played their first concert at a Hallowe'en dance. It was a great success. Later, Bob suggested a change of name and the Boomtown Rats was born. The band title came from the autobiography of American folk singer, Woody Guthrie.

As the Rats' fame grew, Bob used new and startling stunts to attract publicity. At one concert, real rats were let loose among the audience! After a tour of Ireland, they arrived in London in April 1977 where they played the circuit of clubs and pubs. Several record companies approached them, including Virgin Records who offered a million pounds advance payment. However, Bob decided on a smaller company, Ensign, which would grant the band a larger share in future record sales. In 1977 they recorded their first album, *Boomtown Rats*. Their first single, 'Lookin' After No. One', went to No. 11 and earned them an appearance on the BBC's 'Top of the Pops'. Around this time, Bob met Paula Yates whom he later married.

The Rats' second album, *Tonic for the Troops*, was awarded a golden disc. A single, 'Rat Trap', an angry song about urban life, reached No. 1 in November 1978. The Rats had arrived. Their success brought them all over the world. In August 1979 another single, 'I don't like Mondays', also reached No. 1. Bob was very busy, writing songs, making videos, giving interviews, as well as singing. He enjoyed the fame which gave him a platform from which he could speak out, at times shocking people. However, fashions in pop music change rapidly. After three successful years, the band seemed tired and stale. Bob and Paula now had a daughter and money was tight.

One evening in October 1984, as Geldof watched television, what he saw was to transform his life. The BBC showed a film by reporter Michael Buerk about the famine that was devastating Ethiopia. Bob decided to raise money for famine relief by assembling some top-class names in pop music to make a record. Bob worked round the clock on the project, making hundreds of phone calls and attending endless meetings, interviews and programmes. Many famous pop performers agreed to donate their time and services freely. The group was known as Band Aid. 'Do They Know It's Christmas', a song co-written by Bob and Midge Ure, was recorded less than three weeks after the BBC TV documentary. Media coverage was immense and the public response remarkable. The record went straight to No. 1. Eight million copies were sold worldwide. By January 1985, Band Aid had raised over £5 million. Bob, who had promised that every penny would be spent on famine relief, decided to visit Ethiopia. He was devastated by the scale of famine. He was often infuriated by the slow response of officials and politicians to the disaster around them. Millions more would be needed.

Back home in England, Bob had another idea for raising funds for famine relief—a gala concert called Live Aid with a huge gathering of stars televised worldwide. The organisational difficulties would be awesome. Bands on tour all over the world would have to be brought together. Stadiums would be needed to accommodate performers, press and audiences. Television and radio coverage would have to be organised. Transport, catering, advertising, souvenirs, telephone lines to accept money donations, satellite link-ups—the list seemed endless. Once again there was a fantastic response. When 13 July 1985 arrived, two billion people watched a concert unprecedented in the history of popular music.

Towards the end of the concert, Bob handed out copies of 'Do They Know It's Christmas' for the finale. After ten hours, during which the whole planet had sung together, the concert had raised £4 million. Within a week £30 million had been gathered. Ireland's contribution (£7 million in the first two weeks) was superb, donating more per capita than any other country.

By January 1986, £70 million had been raised for famine relief. Bob knew he had to spend the money efficiently on food, medicine, and on a scheme to encourage a better harvest in famine areas in the future. He travelled to Sudan, Ethiopia, Mali, Niger and Chad to assess the situation. The money raised bought 200 trucks, 9 ships and 17,000 tons of grain, as well as helping to build schools, clinics and houses. Band Aid had given countless people hope again. On his return, he made an explosive speech before the European Parliament, attacking Europe's wasteful stockpiles of food. He received many awards and honours during his travels which included being knighted at Buckingham Palace. Meanwhile, the Boomtown Rats went on a final European tour before disbanding.

Bob's autobiography, *Is That It?* (1986), was a bestseller. He was honoured by being nominated for the Nobel Peace Prize in 1986. Slowly he returned to his musical career. In November 1986, he released a solo album, 'Deep in the Heart of Nowhere'. His records sold steadily, with four top-ten hits in Europe. In 1990, another solo album, 'Vegetarians of Love', was released.

Oliver Goldsmith was the son of a Church of Ireland parson. Accounts of his birth vary but an entry in the family Bible mentions that he was born in Pallas, Co. Longford, on 10 November 1728. He was brought up and educated at the village school in Lissoy, Co. Meath, where he showed a flair for music. He loved ballads, played the flute and was fortunate enough to hear the great harpist, Carolan.

School was not a pleasant experience for the boy because he was the butt of jokes due to his small build and ugly features. To compound his problems, his schoolwork showed little promise. At seventeen, he went to Trinity College as a sizar or poor scholar. This meant that, in return for being taught,

he was expected to do odd-jobs around the college. But again Goldsmith neglected his studies, being more interested in music and socialising. However, in 1749 he was given his BA degree. For a while he lived at home with his mother (his father had died), but could not settle down to a job. Deciding to emigrate to America, he travelled to Cork but spent his boat fare before the ship sailed. He then became interested in studying medicine. After studying in Scotland and Holland, however, he decided to earn his living by flute playing. Like a modern day busker, he travelled throughout western Europe, playing for his keep. But when he arrived in England in 1756 he was penniless.

Goldsmith tried many jobs, in a pharmacy, teaching and working for booksellers, before turning to writing articles for magazines and children's stories. He lived in a poor area on the top of Breakneck Steps (so called because they were so dangerous). However, his work for the *Public Ledger* and the publication of his *Chinese Letters* in 1761 made the name Oliver Goldsmith a familiar one in literary society. In 1763, Dr Samuel Johnson asked him to join his influential Literary Club, a group of well-known artists and writers which met in the Turk's Head Tavern, Soho. Goldsmith enjoyed the witty conversations at the club although he himself was a poor talker. His first important poem, 'The Traveller', was well received. In 1766, Goldsmith was rescued from debt by Johnson who sent Goldsmith's novel, *The Vicar of Wakefield*, to a publisher. Goldsmith received £60, a good payment in those days. The book was translated into many languages.

Goldsmith then moved to a better house and turned his hand to stage writing. He enjoyed some success with *The Good-Natur'd Man* (1768) before his classic work, the farce, *She Stoops to Conquer*, appeared in 1773. His most famous poem was the long work, 'The Deserted Village' (1770), whose nostalgic portrait of 'Sweet Auburn! Loveliest village of the plain', was based on his recollections of Lissoy.

Despite his success, Goldsmith was careless with money, living in poverty most of the time. He died of a fever on 4 April 1774 in London, owing debts of £2,000. He had often planned to come home on a visit to his native Ireland, but his sudden death deprived him of the chance. He was buried in a grave in the Temple Churchyards in London, the site of which has since been lost.

OLIVER GOLDSMITH

(1746-1820)

Henry Grattan was born on 3 July 1746. His father was recorder of Dublin, his mother a daughter of a chief justice. After graduating from Trinity College, Dublin, he was admitted to the Middle Temple, London, in 1767 to study law. Grattan spent much time at the gallery in Westminster where he was very impressed by the passionate oratory of his fellow countryman, Edmund Burke.

Grattan returned to Dublin in 1772 and was called to the Irish bar. In 1775, he was offered a vacant parliamentary seat for the borough of Charlemont, Co. Armagh. Grattan's entry into parliament coincided with the decision of Henry Flood, leader of the Irish Patriot Party, to accept government office. Flood believed that this would help him to put pressure on government policy in regard to Ireland. Before long, Grattan took Flood's place as opposition leader. In 1779, Grattan persuaded the British government to remove many restrictions on Irish trade. Three years later, his demand for Irish parliamentary independence, presented at the Dungannon Convention, was granted. A grateful Irish parliament voted a payment of £50,000 to Grattan. After his marriage to Henrietta Fitzgerald he lived at Tinnehinch, Co. Wicklow.

Meanwhile Flood, no longer in office, began to undermine Grattan's leadership. Political differences between the two men climaxed in a bitter argument in the Irish parliament. The two rivals had to be restrained from fighting a duel.

'Grattan's parliament', although easing the voting restrictions against Catholics (they could still not sit in parliament), was limited in representation. The Catholic majority had no members to argue their position; most parliamentary seats were held by patrons; corruption was widespread. Although a Protestant, Grattan was convinced of the necessity of Catholic emancipation. In 1795, however, the recall of the reforming Lord Lieutenant, Lord Fitzwilliam, dashed any hope of further reform. The influence of the French Revolution had created a climate in which violent rebellion was a strong possibility.

In poor health, Grattan was disillusioned by the slow progress of parliamentary change and worried by the growing support for the United Irishmen. He therefore decided to retire from parliament in 1797.

After the unsuccessful Rebellion of 1798, he returned in 1800 as MP for Wicklow to speak against the proposed union of Ireland with Great Britain. However, his efforts failed and he retired again to private life at Tinnehinch. Later, he fought and wounded the Chancellor of the Exchequer, Isaac Corry, who had accused him of aiding the rebellion. In 1805, he represented the English borough of Malton at Westminster and the following year he represented Dublin. Grattan now concentrated his political energies on Catholic emancipation. But in 1819 his health began to deteriorate. Following a journey to London the following year, he died on 4 June 1820.

Henry Grattan, principal architect of the Irish parliament 1782–1800 (often known as 'Grattan's Parliament'), was buried in Westminster Abbey in London. His speeches were published by his son in 1820.

Grattan addressing the Irish House of Commons

(1852-1932)

Isabella Augusta Persse was born on 15 March 1832 at Roxborough House, Co. Galway. Educated at home, she was inspired by the folklore, ballads, poetry and rebel stories told by her Irish-speaking nurse, Mary Sheridan. Although anxious to learn Irish herself, Isabella was told it was no language for a lady.

In 1880 she married Sir William Gregory who was thirty-five years older. Lady Gregory travelled widely with him and visited such countries as Egypt, Spain, India and Ceylon. After his death in 1892, she edited his life story. In 1882, she published a pamphlet defending an Egyptian revolt against Turkish rule. She was also involved in raising funds for a poor London parish and supporting cottage industries in Ireland. Lady Gregory spoke out against Gladstone's Home Rule Bill.

Believing that Ireland must be rescued from English misgovernment, she was involved in the centenary celebrations of the 1798 Fenian Rising. She published five volumes of folk-tales and history between 1906 and 1920.

In 1898, Lady Gregory met the poet and playwright, William Butler Yeats. His visit to her gracious home in Coole Park, near Gort, was the beginning of a lifelong friendship which led to the foundation of the Irish Literary Theatre. She organised a local branch of the Gaelic League and began taking Irish lessons. Lady Gregory's work with Yeats, Martyn Moore and the Fay brothers led to the foundation of the Abbey Theatre. It opened on 27 December 1904 with a production of her comedy, *Spreading the News*, as well as Yeats's *On Baile's Strand*.

Lady Gregory wrote thirty plays, including comedies such as *The Rising of the Moon* (1907) and a historical play, *Kincora* (1905). These works showed her sense of realism and mischievous humour. She was an energetic worker, writing plays, directing productions, advising actors and helping to manage the theatre from day to day. A director of the Abbey until her death, she encouraged talented writers such as Synge, Shaw, Hyde and O'Casey. She also helped Yeats when he had problems with plot and dialogue in his plays. Her home, Coole Park, was a meeting place for leading writers and artists of the time. In 1909, she courageously insisted that George Bernard Shaw's play, *The Shewing Up Of Blanco Posnet*, which had been banned in England, should be staged in Dublin.

The Abbey Theatre Company went on tour throughout Ireland and established a fine reputation. In 1910 the theatre toured America with Synge's play, *The Playboy of the Western World*. Showing an Ireland which was different from what the Irish-Americans imagined, it caused riots in several cities. At one stage, the cast was thrown into prison!

During World War I, Lady Gregory's only son, Major Robert Gregory, was killed in France, a death commemorated in verse by the poet W. B. Yeats.

Lady Gregory was involved in many important issues including the Lane Collection controversy. After the death of her nephew, Hugh Lane, she campaigned for his picture collection to be returned to Ireland from London.

Roxborough House was burned down during the Irish Civil War and Coole Park was sold to the Land Commission in 1927. However, Lady Gregory occupied her home and garden until her death on 22 May 1932.

Lady Gregory's home, Coole Park, Gort, Co. Galway

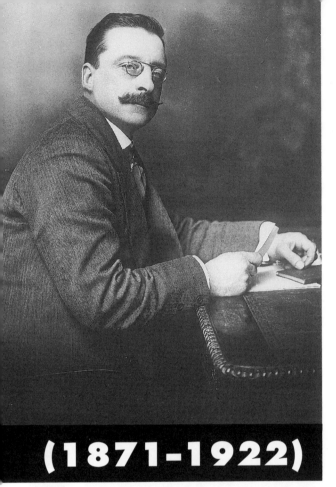

(1871-1922)

Arthur Griffith was born on 31 March 1871 at Upper Dominick Street, Dublin. His father was a printer, so after attending Strand Street Christian Brothers School, Arthur was apprenticed to the printing trade. Already his interest in Irish nationalism was being nourished by membership of the Irish Republican Brotherhood and the Gaelic League. He went to South Africa in 1896 for reasons of health and edited an English weekly newspaper in the Transvaal. The paper soon ceased publication, however, due to Griffith's editorial stance which supported the Boers in their struggle against the British. Abandoning journalism, he worked in the goldmines for a while before returning to Dublin in 1898. There, he was invited by his friend, Willie Rooney, to become editor of a new weekly paper, *The United Irishman*. After the death of Charles Stewart Parnell, the immediate prospect of advancing the cause of Irish independence by parliamentary methods was in tatters. Griffith wrote a number of articles proposing that Irish members of parliament should no longer attend Westminster. Instead, he said they should set up their own national assembly in Dublin. These articles, republished in 1904 as *The Resurrection of Hungary*, *A Parallel for Ireland*, cited the case of Hungarian independence from Austria which had been achieved when Hungarian parliamentarians refused to attend the parliament in Vienna.

Having formed the National Council in 1905, Griffith further explained his ideas at the organisation's annual convention two years later. His policy, known as Sinn Féin ('Ourselves'), preached national self-reliance. In 1906, with *The United Irishman* closing down, he started a new paper, *Sinn Féin*. A Sinn Féin Party soon developed in 1911 with Griffith as its president. Disappointed at the concessions offered to Irish nationalistic ambitions in the Home Rule Bill of 1912, Griffith joined the Irish Volunteers to counter Unionist opposition to Home Rule. He was involved in landing weapons for the Volunteers at Howth in July 1914. Griffith's paper was suppressed as a result. Although he was not actively involved in the 1916 Rising, his writings promoting Irish self-reliance were considered dangerous and he was imprisoned along with the revolutionaries.

Following the execution of the 1916 leaders, Éamon de Valera became President of Sinn Féin the following year. On a wave of public support, Sinn Féin had a spectacular victory in the 1918 general election, with Griffith being elected in East Cavan. The elected Sinn Féiners, following Griffith's policy of absenteeism from Westminster, met in Dublin for the first Dáil in 1919. Griffith was elected Vice-president of the new Republic and Minister for Home Affairs. However, he could not prevent the use of force which soon escalated into the War of Independence against British occupation. During the negotiations for the Anglo-Irish Treaty, Griffith led the Irish delegation in London. Although de Valera opposed the terms of the agreement, the Dáil supported it and Griffith was elected President of the Dáil. He later became President of the new Irish Free State. June 1922 saw the outbreak of civil war. Griffith, exhausted by his labours, died of a cerebral haemorrhage in Dublin on 12 August 1922 and was buried in Glasnevin Cemetery, Dublin.

(1725-1803)

Arthur Guinness was born in 1725 at Celbridge, Co. Kildare. He was the eldest son of Richard Guinness who was a land steward for Dr Price, Church of Ireland Archbishop of Cashel. Richard Guinness brewed beer for tenants and labourers working on the estate.

Little is known about Guinness's early life. But when Dr Price died in 1752, he left Arthur £100 which helped him to start up his brewing business. By 1756 he was running a brewery in Leixlip. Dismayed by the crippling export restrictions and heavy taxation on brewing, Guinness considered emigrating to Wales at one stage. However, in 1759 he moved to St James's Gate in Dublin, leaving his brother to manage the brewery in Leixlip. At St James's Gate, Guinness started the business that has remained in the Guinness family ever since. It was a popular location for brewing because it was near to the city water supply. In 1761 he married Olivia Whitmore, a relative of Henry Grattan.

Eighteenth-century breweries, unlike huge modern ones, were small. Most county towns had their own brewery which was often attached to a public house. This meant that the beer could be produced and sold in one place. In 1798, Guinness began to extend his market by sending his produce on barges along Ireland's new canals. Beer, often called ale, was a popular drink, but Guinness also brewed porter, a darker type of beer containing roasted barley. Porter got its name from the fact that it was originally drunk by the porters at the London markets. Later a stronger porter was brewed called 'stouter porter' which became known as 'stout'.

Guinness was faced with a problem when the government taxed the brewers on their products in order to raise money. This forced the price of beer upwards and made it too expensive for many ordinary people. During a debate in the Irish House of Commons, Guinness condemned the harsh new taxes. Supported by Henry Grattan, who was a persuasive speaker and also a relation, Guinness succeeded in having the tax on beer abolished in 1795. It was a victory warmly welcomed by Irish brewers.

Arthur Guinness was also involved in a quarrel with Dublin City Council over water rights. When the waterworks committee tried to fill in a water channel from which his brewery received its supply, Guinness sent them away with a pickaxe in his hands. After many years of legal dispute, both sides came to an agreement in 1785.

Guinness bought a fine country house in Beaumont, Dublin, where he lived with his wife and large family. Altogether he had twenty-one children, of whom ten survived. He was always busy extending his brewery, building flour mills at Kilmainham and also working to improve conditions in Irish prisons. He also started the first Sunday school in Ireland in 1786.

Arthur Guinness continued managing his brewery business until old age, helped by his sons, Arthur and Benjamin. Retiring to Beaumont, he died on 23 January 1803 and was buried near Kill, Co. Kildare, leaving his son, Arthur, in charge. In time, the Guinness brewery grew to be the largest in Europe and the biggest exporter of stout in the world, occupying over sixty acres in Dublin.

The Guinness group of companies is now established worldwide. It is involved in many diversified products and activities, including a publishing house which produces the ever popular *Guinness Book of Records*.

(1805-1865)

William Rowan Hamilton, a solicitor's son, was born at 36 Lower Dominick Street, Dublin, on 4 August 1805. His father had given him the name Rowan after Hamilton Rowan, a leader of the 1798 Rebellion. A child prodigy, he was taught by his uncle, a clergyman, at Trim, Co. Meath. By the age of seven he could read Hebrew. When he was twelve he had a knowledge of Arabic, Hindustani, Malay, Persian and Sanskrit, as well as modern European and classic languages. At fourteen years of age he composed a welcome in Persian for the Ambassador of Persia who was visiting Dublin. It was evident that he was a genius. Hamilton began to teach himself mathematics, and by the age of seventeen he had detected an error in Laplace's *Mecanique Celeste*, a classic work in astronomy, and had mastered Newton's theories. At the age of eighteen he entered Trinity College, Dublin. During his second year there, a paper which he read to the Royal Irish Academy was published as a treatise, *Theory of Systems of Rays* (1828). In 1827, although still an undergraduate, Hamilton became professor of astronomy at Trinity and Astronomer Royal at Dunsink Observatory in Finglas, Dublin. As secretary to the British Association for the Advancement of Science which visited Dublin in 1835, he was knighted for his services to astronomy.

His *General Method in Dynamics*, published in 1834, was well received throughout Europe. His studies won him an honorary membership of the Academy of St Petersburg, an honour seldom awarded to non-Russians. As well as membership of many great European scientific academies, Hamilton was an ambassador for science for his country. In 1837 Hamilton became President of the Royal Irish Academy. He was also the first foreign member of the National Academy of Sciences in America.

International acclaim continued to mark his progress. Hamilton received gold medals from the Royal Society for work on optics and dynamics. However, his interest was turning to the field of pure mathematics. On 16 October 1843, while crossing over the Royal Canal in Dublin with his wife, he suddenly rushed to the stone parapet of Brougham bridge and began carving on it a row of letters and numbers with a penknife. This was his famous formula for Quaternions on which he had been working. It was one of the most important discoveries ever in mathematics and had practical applications for problems in astronomy, engineering and electricity.

Hamilton wrote a huge number of papers on mathematical issues, the most famous being *Lectures on Quaternions*, begun at Trinity in 1848 and published in 1853. His best-known work, *The Elements of Quaternions*, kept him preoccupied until his death in Dublin on 2 September 1865. The work was edited by his son for posthumous publication in 1866.

Although he was obsessed with mathematics, Hamilton loved poetry and wrote many sonnets. He was friendly with many of the leading English writers of the time, including William Wordsworth and Maria Edgeworth. He accompanied Wordsworth on his Irish journey. Hamilton's verse is to be found in many nineteenth-century anthologies.

WILLIAM HAMILTON

(1925-   )

Charles Haughey was born on 16 September 1925 in Castlebar, Co. Mayo. His father, an army officer, retired first to Co. Meath when Haughey was three. Before long, the family moved to Donnycarney in Dublin. The youngster went to Scoil Mhuire, Marino, and later attended St Joseph's Christian Brothers School, Fairview. A keen sportsman, he played Gaelic games for St Vincent's and also for Parnell's clubs (winning with the latter a Dublin Senior Football Championship medal in 1945).

While studying commerce at University College, Dublin, Haughey met his wife, Maureen, daughter of a future Taoiseach, Seán Lemass. They were married in 1951 and have a family of one daughter and three sons.

In 1946, he graduated from UCD. After considering following his father's footsteps into an army career (while working as a chartered accountant he became a lieutenant in the FCA), he was persuaded by his family to go into business. With his friend Harry Boland, he set up the accountancy firm of Haughey, Boland and Company. Through his association with Boland, he became a member of Fianna Fáil in 1949. Following two unsuccessful attempts, he won a seat in Dáil Éireann in March 1957, representing the constituency of Dublin North East.

Haughey's rise to prominence was a rapid one, becoming parliamentary secretary to the Minister for Justice in 1960. In 1961, he became Minister for Justice in Seán Lemass's government and was much respected for his energy and ability. His achievements included the Succession Act which gave wives a right to share the family income, and the ending of the death penalty for all except capital crimes. Three years later, he was appointed Minister for Agriculture and Fisheries. He faced an aggressive campaign for higher milk prices, during which protesting farmers camped outside his office. Although refusing to bow to pressure, he later secured a price rise from the Cabinet.

In 1966, Haughey became Minister for Finance at a time of economic growth and optimism. His concern for the disadvantaged in society brought about major changes in official attitudes to social welfare. It resulted in measures providing the elderly with free transport, telephones and electricity, as well as TV and radio licences. Other far-reaching steps included a tax-free scheme for writers and artists (1969) which reflected his own lifelong interest in and patronage of the arts. Allowances were given to deserted wives for the first time, and children living in rural areas were given free school transport.

In 1970, Haughey was charged with attempting to import arms into the state, the weapons destined to help the nationalist community in Northern Ireland. Although dismissed from the Cabinet, he was found not guilty in the subsequent Arms Trial. Displaying memorable resilience and determination, he spent his years of political exile well. He patiently rebuilt his political career, cultivated nationwide contacts and friendships throughout the Fianna Fáil organisation and slowly built up a base for a return to power.

By January 1975, Haughey was Fianna Fáil spokesman on health. Now living in Kinsealy, Co. Dublin, he also bought Inishvickillane, one of Kerry's Blasket Islands, as a holiday retreat. When Fianna Fáil won the 1977 general election, he was appointed Minister for Health and Social Welfare by the Taoiseach, Jack Lynch. His was a busy ministry. It included the Family Planning Act which legalised the sale of contraceptives for married couples, the introduction of PRSI, the opening of several new hospitals, and restrictions on cigarette advertising.

On 7 December 1979 following Lynch's resignation, Haughey became leader of Fianna Fáil. Four days later, he was elected Taoiseach, only nine years after being dismissed from Cabinet. However, factors including a worsening economic situation, rising unemployment and tensions in Northern Ireland leading to the death on hunger strike of Republican prisoners weakened his government, letting a coalition of Fine Gael and Labour come to power in June 1981.

In March 1982, Haughey became Taoiseach again, forming a government with the support of the Workers Party and independent deputies. Handicapped by a series of internal difficulties and other potential controversies, this regime came to an abrupt end in November of the same year with another Fine Gael/ Labour coalition returning to power. In 1984, he played a major role in the New Ireland Forum at which constitutional nationalist parties in Ireland proposed various political models for Northern Ireland. He indicated his preference for a unified state. Allegations concerning the tapping of journalists' telephones and challenges to his leadership led to the formation of a new political party, the Progressive Democrats, in November 1985.

Returning to power in a minority government (March 1987), he launched the Programme for National Recovery with unions and employers in the hope of ushering in an era of financial order. The agreement was renegotiated in 1991. Speaking at the United Nations in June 1988, Haughey declared that the only

CHARLES J. HAUGHEY

acceptable level of nuclear weaponry was zero.

In June 1989, outright electoral success eluded him yet again, with Fianna Fáil winning only seventy-seven seats. Political necessity overcoming reluctance, he made party history by forming a coalition with the Progressive Democrats.

In 1990, as President of the EC Council of Ministers, Haughey chaired important meetings on the issues of European political/economic union and on German reunification. His presidency was seen as a particularly successsful one. In December 1991, with his eleven EC partners, he negotiated the European Union Treaty at Maastricht in Holland. Following a series of events which tested his legendary survival skills to the full (including the dismissal of several Cabinet colleagues, a rash of financial scandals involving state companies and the re-emergence of the 1982 phone-tapping affair), he resigned as Taoiseach in February 1992, having signed the final draft of the European Union Treaty.

(1939-   )

Seamus Heaney was born on 13 April 1939, the eldest of nine children. Home was the family farm at Bellaghy in south Co. Derry. At primary school, Heaney developed an early love of poetry, learning to recite passages from Byron and Keats. In 1951, the youngster won a scholarship to St Columb's College, Derry, as a boarder. From there another scholarship enabled him to attend Belfast's Queen's University where he took a first-class honours BA degree in English. His first poetic efforts were published in the University magazine under the tentative pen-name, 'Incertus'. Under the stewardship of the English critic, Philip Hobsbaum, a group of writers, including Michael and Edna Longley, Seamus Deane, James Simmons, Stewart Parker, Heaney himself and his future wife, Marie Devlin, met weekly, exercising and refining their craft.

With his student days behind him, Heaney became an English teacher at St Joseph's Technical College, Belfast. His work appeared regularly in papers and journals throughout Ireland. *Death of a Naturalist*, his first collection of verse, was published in 1966. In it, themes of loss, menace, decay and the passing of innocence are examined against a rural background.

Heaney was by then a married man (they now have three children). He lectured in English at Queen's University as well as writing articles and reviews for the prestigious *Listener* magazine. In 1969, *Door into the Dark*, his second volume of verse, appeared. From autumn 1970 to the following summer, he worked as a visiting lecturer at the University of California at Berkeley. There, he absorbed a rich mosaic of ethnic writing as well as a new world of free-verse techniques, some of which filtered into his own work and were evident in his next volume, *Wintering Out* (1972).

These were years of political turbulence and terrorist violence in Northern Ireland. In this cramped province of tension, Heaney, now a literary landmark, feared he might be pressurised into adopting a rigid political stance. Resigning from Queen's, he took his family to live in Ashford, Co. Wicklow, in 1973. There he began translating a medieval Irish poem, 'Buile Shiubhne Geti', which he entitled, 'Sweeney Astray'. In 1975, *North*, his fourth collection, appeared. In this work, Heaney explored the Norse tradition in Ireland, counterpointing the victims of sectarian strife in Northern Ireland with ancient rites of sacrifice.

Heaney's name was now a regular, even expected, inclusion in anthologies of verse, journals and magazines. In 1978, he was appointed head of the English department in Carysfort Teacher Training College in Dublin.

Field Work (1979), his fifth collection, is a tightly written work, employing traditional forms of sonnet and elegy in classical metre and diction. 1980 saw the publication of prose pieces entitled *Preoccupations*.

In 1982, Heaney was granted a five-year contract as resident poet at Harvard University, Boston, spending four months annually on campus. In 1982, *The Rattle Bag* was published. In 1984,

he was elected to the Boylston Chair of Rhetoric and Oratory at Harvard.

Recent works include: *Station Island* (1984), a penitential work in which the pilgrim poet encounters the ghosts of friends and famous writers; *Selected Poems* (1965/1975/1988); *The Haw Lantern* (1987); a play, *No Cure at Troy* (1990), Heaney's version of *Philoctetes* by the Greek playwright, Sophocles; and *Seeing Things* (1991).

Heaney's reputation is worldwide and his work has been translated into several languages. He is a tireless ambassador for poetry in Ireland, most recently developing contacts with writers throughout eastern Europe and South America. In 1989 he was bestowed the prestigious Chair of Poetry at Oxford University.

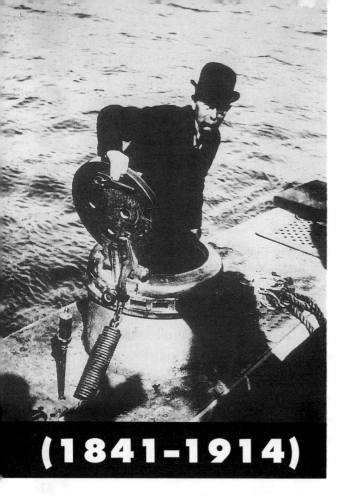

(1841-1914)

John Philip Holland, born in Castle Street, Liscannor, Co. Clare, on 24 February 1841, was the son of a coast-guard. He went to the Christian Brothers School in Ennistymon and later to their school in Limerick. Impressed by their contribution to Irish education, Holland decided to join the Order and took his first vows in 1858. He then pursued a teaching career in Christian Brothers schools in Cork, Portlaoise, Enniscorthy, Drogheda and Dundalk. In 1872, however, he was released from his vows, emigrated to America and took up a teaching position in New Jersey.

For years, Holland had nursed the idea of an underwater vessel. Indeed as early as 1870 he had completed the first plans for his invention. After much patient experimentation which was funded by Irish contacts, he built a small functioning submarine. Although his design was rejected by the US Navy in 1875, his invention attracted the interest of the Irish Republican group, Clan na Gael, who saw possibilities in Holland's model as a weapon against the British Navy. They supported his experiments and gave him money to build two submarines.

Holland's first submarine, built shortly after his arrival in America, looked like a long narrow cigar. It was operated by a man using pedals to turn the propeller. Holland decided to test the craft himself. The first boat tested on the Passaic River in 1878 was a failure. However, the success of his second model, *The Fenian Ram*, in 1881 set out the blueprint for the basic features of future submarines. *The Ram*, a 30-foot craft carrying three men, travelled at seven mph above water. It also had a tube from which explosives could be fired underwater.

Power was a major problem. Steam, compressed air and electricity had all been tried by previous inventors with little success. Steering was also difficult to control below water. There was also trouble with the intense pressure of water on the sides of a craft, the air supply for crew and, of course, the installation of a weapon system for use in naval warfare.

In 1888, the US Navy, impressed by improvements in Holland's designs, asked him to submit plans. In 1895 he was awarded a US government contract to build a ship. However, the project failed, partly due to the fact that the Navy interfered with his design. In order to demonstrate that his own model could work, Holland built the *Holland*, launching it successfully in 1898. The navy bought the *Holland* in 1900 and commissioned him to build six more submarines. Holland had by then refined his model which had a speed of seven knots on the surface, six below. It was powered with a petrol engine, could travel fifty miles at a time below water and could dive to twenty-eight feet within five seconds. It carried torpedoes and dynamite shells. At this stage the periscope had not been designed, so visibility was maintained by portholes in the ship's hull.

The *Holland* (Mark 9) became the USS *Holland*, the first submarine in the American navy. Other governments became interested, and in 1901 five ships were ordered for the British admiralty—a strange customer, considering Holland's earliest patrons! Soon, Holland's submarines were sailing in the navies of Russia, Japan and several other powerful countries. By World War I, nearly sixty submarines were in action, most of them built to John Holland's design.

A perfectionist, Holland kept striving to improve his invention. In 1904 he built a respirator which allowed crew members to escape from damaged submarines trapped underwater.

Holland himself, although he received many rich contracts, died in poverty because of business problems. The father of the modern submarine died in New Jersey on 12 August 1914, just before his major invention proved its deadly usefulness in World War I.

(1911-1986)

Monsignor James Horan was born in Partry, Co. Mayo, on 5 May 1911. From an early age, he had a love of the Irish language, often spending his holidays in nearby Irish-speaking Tourmakeady. For a while he toyed with the idea of becoming an engineer (his father was a builder). But after winning a scholarship to St Jarlath's, Tuam, Co. Galway, he went on to St Patrick's College, Maynooth, Ireland's major seminary. A brilliant student, he took Celtic Studies as his primary degree and received first-class honours when he was ordained in 1936.

He was first appointed to Pollackshans parish in Glasgow. After a few months he worked in Cardonald before settling for three years in Dumbarton, the most Catholic parish in Scotland. The young Irish curate enjoyed his life there among his generous parishioners. During his final year in Dumbarton he served as chaplain on board the liner *California* which was sailing to America. It was the first of many subsequent trips to the United States.

Recalled to Ireland in 1939, he served in Ballyglunin, Co. Mayo, and then in Carraroe, Connemara, where his fluency in Irish was a great asset. His next appointment was to Tooreen, near Ballyhaunis, Co. Mayo, where his energy and flair for business resulted in the building of a dance hall. The Tooreen dance hall attracted patrons from all over Connacht. It also gave a much-needed boost to the social and economic life of the village.

Fr Horan's next post was the village of Cloonfad on the borders of Mayo, Roscommon and Galway. Here again, his organisational talents were exercised. Through his persistent demands, government approval was granted for 1,200 acres of forest to be planted in the area, giving local employment. He also persuaded the County Council to improve the roads around the village.

In 1963 he was made curate of Knock, a small Mayo village famed for the apparition of Our Lady in 1879. Four years later, Fr Horan was appointed Administrator of Knock and Director of the Shrine. Even though Knock was a focal point for pilgrims from all over the world, its facilities were poor. Recognising these deficiencies, he set to work with his customary drive, and over the next few years transformed the village. He was the mastermind behind all the modern developments there, including the great basilica, the resthouse for resident invalids, a rest and care centre for day invalids, a confessional chapel, a processional square, large-scale parking facilities, a social services centre and a marriage bureau.

In 1979, the year in which Pope John Paul II arrived in Knock to celebrate its centenary, James Horan was appointed Monsignor.

In 1981 his ambitious plan to build an airport, both to serve the shrine and to boost business in the region, received government approval. However, when a subsequent government refused to give further financial assistance after £9 million had been spent, the project seemed doomed. But the Monsignor refused to give in. He spearheaded an amazing series of fundraising drives. Eventually, despite political opposition and much scepticism, Connacht Regional Airport was opened in May 1986. As chairman of the airport board, Monsignor Horan was deeply involved in the negotiations between statutory bodies and international aviation authorities. For his efforts he was made Mayo Man of the Year.

He died in his sleep on a pilgrimage to Lourdes on 1 August 1986. His body was flown home to his own airport where, days previously, he had welcomed the first flight from Washington. He is buried in the grounds of the basilica, which he himself built.

(1937-   )

John Hume was born on 18 January 1937 at 20 Lower Nassau Street in the north side of Derry city. He was the eldest of seven children and received his early education at St Eugene Boys' School. A scholarship to St Columb's, the local Catholic grammar school, opened up a new world to him. An enthusiastic player of soccer, Gaelic football and cricket, Hume studied hard as well, winning a scholarship for the priesthood at St Patrick's College, Maynooth, where he studied history, logic and French. However, in 1957, after being hospitalised, he failed to sit his BA honours exams. Deciding against the priesthood, he left St Patrick's and eventually turned to teaching. During this time he worked on his MA thesis which dealt with the social and economic history of Derry from 1825 to 1850.

Returning to Derry, he saw the need for a community banking system and formed the Derry Credit Union in the Bogside in 1960. From humble origins, the movement spread. By 1984, it had assets of over four million pounds, and ninety-four branches. It became the largest community credit union in the world. During the same year, he married Patricia Hone, a local girl. They have five children.

A skilled debater, Hume's involvement in local causes soon made him a popular public figure. In 1964, he made his first television appearance in a discussion entitled, 'Target Derry'. After this, he scripted a film for BBC as part of the city's Arts Festival. In 1967, he was a joint-founder of Derry's Housing Association. In the mid-1960s he also embarked on a short business career, setting up Atlantic Harvest, a firm which marketed smoked salmon from Lough Foyle. He persuaded the mighty Cunard cruise line to become a customer.

John Hume came to political prominence in the civil rights movement in Derry in 1968. He was vice-chairman of the Derry Citizen's Action Committee, 1968–69, when riots and marches brought the world's media to Northern Ireland. Hume's support for non-violent protest, along with his reasoned denunciation against discrimination, made him an international figure.

Standing as an independent for Northern Ireland's parliament (Stormont), Hume was elected for the Foyle constituency in 1969. The following year, he co-founded the Social Democratic and Labour Party (SDLP). Elected deputy leader of the SDLP in 1973, he soon emerged as the party's chief policy maker.

Hume served on the Northern Ireland Assembly from 1973 to 1974. He played a crucial part in the Sunningdale Agreement which led to the establishment of the power-sharing Executive. Appointed Head of Commerce in the new Executive, he was deeply involved with the economic repercussions of the Loyalist strike which broke the Agreement. During these years he built up important contacts with high-ranking US politicians, looking to America as a lever to create political movement in Northern Ireland. He also became adviser on consumer affairs and transport to the EEC Commissioner, Richard Burke.

In 1979, Hume was elected to the European Parliament. He was now leader of his party, succeeding Gerry Fitt. Hume called for a council for a New Ireland. In it, politicians from the Republic and Northern Ireland would come up with a blueprint for Irish unity. Hume's proposal led to the New Ireland Forum. In 1983, he became the first non-Unionist to be elected to Westminster from Derry and was re-elected in 1984 as a Member of the European Parliament (MEP). The 1985 Anglo-Irish Agreement was a product of much political pressure on the part of Hume. He saw the Agreement as a clear signal to Unionists that the position of Nationalists must be respected, and that Irish unity would have to respect

Unionism. In 1988, Hume led his party into discussions with Northern Ireland's Secretary of State on local government. He also participated in controversial meetings with Sinn Féin which were aimed at ending the constant cycle of violence and reprisal. Earlier, in 1985, he had also been involved in discussions with the Provisional IRA, incurring the wrath of Unionists. His appeal to Unionists at the 1988 SDLP Annual Conference to meet for discussions parallel to the Anglo-Irish Agreement met with rejection.

Hume's consummate political skills, his consistent, calmly stated commitment to non-violence and his extensive contacts guarantee him an important role in any future developments in Northern Irish politics.

(1860-1949)

Douglas Hyde was born near Castlerea, Co. Roscommon, on 17 January 1860. Except for a brief period's schooling in Dublin, he was taught at home by his father, the Protestant rector at Frenchpark, Co. Roscommon. At that time, Irish was commonly spoken in the Frenchpark area and the young boy grew up hearing Irish spoken by the local country people. Hyde went to Trinity College, Dublin, in 1880 where he was a distinguished student, winning prizes for literature studies.

Douglas Hyde studied for a while to become a Church of Ireland clergyman, but turned to law instead, graduating in 1884. He joined the Society for the Preservation of the Irish Language and also helped to establish the *Gaelic Union Journal*, the first Irish periodical. Hyde's linguistic ability was enormous. He was competent in German, Hebrew, Latin, Greek and French, as well as Irish and English. In 1889 he published a collection of folk-tales, and the following year wrote another book of stories, *Beside the Fire*. This was followed in 1891 with the Irish edition, *Cois na Tine*. He also published many poems in Irish. For these he used the pen-name 'An Craoibhín Aoibhinn' ('delightful little branch') by which he became well known.

After a short period spent teaching English in Canada, Hyde returned to Ireland in 1892. He married in 1893 and settled down at Ratra Park, Co. Roscommon. Hyde devoted all his time to the restoration of Irish as an everyday language throughout the country. In autumn 1892, he delivered a lecture to the Royal Literary Society, of which he was president, emphasising the need for the 'Gaelicisation' of Ireland. He toured the countryside, with the intention of collecting folk-tales which he felt should be preserved. Hyde's most famous book was *Love Songs of Connacht* (1893), a collection of Irish and English poems, some of them his own.

The last decade of the nineteenth century was an exciting period of cultural awakening in Ireland, with great activity in politics, language and the arts. Hyde was concerned that Ireland might lose its unique identity and adopt a totally English culture. To achieve his aim of national restoration, he established the Gaelic League in 1893. Hyde became the League's first president, a post he held until his retirement in 1915.

The Gaelic League was open to all. It promoted the cause of Irish language, culture and games, as well as local industries. By 1905, the League had branches nationwide. Through the Irish language lessons it provided, thousands of people began to speak Irish. Hyde persuaded the British government to provide money for the teaching of Irish in primary schools. He also argued for its inclusion as a subject in the secondary school curriculum. Against much opposition, he campaigned to have Irish accepted as a compulsory subject for entry to the new National University.

All this time, Hyde was writing and collecting material. His play, *Casadh an tSúgáin*, was the first play in Irish to be presented on a professional stage (1901).

In 1905, Hyde toured the US to raise funds for the League and collected the then huge sum of £11,000. In 1908 he was appointed the first professor of Modern Irish at the National University of Ireland, a position he held until 1932.

As the campaign for full Irish independence grew, Hyde did his best to keep his League clear of politics. However, in 1915, when the League committee decided to include support for independence among its aims, Hyde resigned.

In 1925 he became a senator. In 1938, Hyde was unanimously elected first President of Ireland. Old but still energetic, he served his full term until 1945. He died on 12 July 1949 and was buried in the family burial ground near Frenchpark.

(1951-   )

Neil Jordan was born in Sligo on 25 February 1951. He was educated in Dublin at Belgrove National School, Clontarf, and at St Paul's School, Raheny. He later studied English and History in University College, Dublin.

As a teenager, Jordan had become involved in writing, directing and acting with the city centre theatre Slot Players (the brainchild of Jim and Peter Sheridan). He renewed contact with the Sheridan brothers later when, after a period in England, he joined them in a project called the Children's T-Company. This was Dublin's first street theatre group which also played to Dublin school audiences.

By now, Jordan was making his name as a writer. He was co-founder of the Irish Writers Co-operative which published his first book, *Nights in Tunisia* (1978). This brilliant collection of short stories won him the *Guardian* prize a year later. He also wrote two novels, *The Past* (1980) and *The Dream of a Beast* (1983).

At this stage, Jordan was also writing for television. A play, *Miracles and Miss Langan*, was transmitted on BBC radio and later filmed by RTE. He wrote a script, 'Travellers', in 1980. However he had to surrender artistic control on the project and was disappointed in the way it was filmed. Following his documentary on the making of John Boorman's film, *Excalibur* (1981), Jordan was finally in the position of being able to direct his own work with *Angel* (1982) which was set against the backdrop of troubles in Northern Ireland. Having raised the money from Channel 4 and the Irish Film Board, Jordan chose Stephen Rea and Honor Heffernan to play the leading roles. *Angel* was a marvellously assured directing début which won an award at the Cannes film festival. *The Company of Wolves* (1984) which won Jordan the Best Director award in the British Critics Circle (1984) and *Mona Lisa* (1985) marked him as a unique talent behind the camera. Bob Hoskins took the Best Actor award at Cannes for his portrayal of the soft-hearted gangster in *Mona Lisa*. Next, Jordan wrote and directed a farce, *High Spirits* (1988). To his frustration, it was re-edited without his knowledge and unfavourably received, although it was commercially successful in the United States.

Jordan's next venture was to direct *We're No Angels*, starring Robert De Niro and Sean Penn (1989). Despite the impressive cast, the film failed to satisfy the high expectations generated. Recently, he returned to Co. Wicklow to write and direct *The Miracle* (1991). The film, starring Beverly D'Angelo and Donal McCann, concerns a son who falls in love with the mother he thought was dead.

Jordan is an individualistic director. He is fiercely independent and unafraid of experimentation. He rejected the invitation to direct the popular Tom Cruise picture, *Cocktail*, and the remake of *DOA* starring Denis Quaid. Instead, he chose to pursue his own artistic vision. His latest film, *A Soldier's Wife*, got under way in November 1991.

NEIL JORDAN

(1882-1941)

James Joyce was born at 41 Brighton Square, Rathgar, Dublin, on 2 February 1882. He was the eldest in a family of ten. Because of financial difficulties in the family, the Joyces were forced to move frequently from one house to another. Their problems increased in 1893 when James's father lost his job as an official in the Tax Office. They then moved into lodgings in the poorer side of Dublin city.

In 1888, at the age of six, Joyce was sent as a boarder to Clongowes Wood College, Co. Kildare. Three years later, he had to leave as his father could not afford the fees. He continued his education in Belvedere College on the northside of Dublin. Joyce was a fine student and from 1898 he studied languages at University College,

Dublin, learning Latin, Italian, French, German and Norwegian. He published articles and essays in the university magazine. His first published work on the Norwegian playwright, Ibsen, was published in 1900.

On leaving college, Joyce decided to study medicine in Paris, but in 1903 he had to return to Dublin as his mother was dying. He then stayed in Dublin searching for employment, writing poems and stories. Joyce was also a fine singer. In 1904, he finished third in the tenor competition at the Feis Cheoil. Joyce also taught for a while at Clifton School, Dalkey, and lived in a Martello tower by the sea at Sandycove.

In 1904 Joyce left Ireland. He felt that Dublin life was a prison of dull conformity and that he would only develop himself fully as a writer if he went abroad. Together with a Galway girl, Nora Barnacle, who later became his wife, Joyce lived in Switzerland and Italy where he earned a living teaching English. His book, *Dubliners*, a collection of short stories, was finally published in 1914. The final story in *Dubliners*, 'The Dead', is considered to be one of literature's greatest short stories. Joyce then began writing *A Portrait of the Artist as a Young Man* (1916) which told his own life story up to leaving Ireland.

Returning to Ireland for a brief visit in 1909, Joyce opened a cinema, Dublin's first, in Mary Street. It was called the Volta, but it failed as a business venture. With his wife and two children, he visited Ireland for the last time in 1912. After a disagreement with his Dublin publisher over *Dubliners*, he left, never to return. Although an exile,

Dublin was constantly in his thoughts. Gifted with a marvellous memory, he could describe every shop and building in certain Dublin streets. In 1918 he wrote *Exiles*, a play.

Joyce devoted his later life to two outstanding books—*Ulysses* and *Finnegans Wake*. *Ulysses* narrates the separate and shared experience of two men through the course of one day, 16 June 1904. Although difficult on first reading, it is a fascinating and enjoyable picture of Dublin life. Since its publication by Sylvia Beach in 1922, *Ulysses* has been translated into many languages and is acknowledged as a classic of modern literature. In 1927, a slim volume of poetry,

Pomes Pennyeach (1927), was published in Paris.

Finnegans Wake (1939) is a puzzling work. It is written in a language invented by Joyce, in which he borrowed from several other languages. It took Joyce seventeen years to complete the book before it was published in 1939, confirming his worldwide reputation.

As Joyce grew older, his eyesight, which was never strong, deteriorated, making him nearly blind. He had twenty-five operations on his eyes, calling himself at one stage, 'an international eyesore'! James Joyce died in Zurich on 13 January 1941. He was buried there, in Fluntern Cemetery.

(1904-1967)

Patrick Kavanagh was born in Iniskeen, Co. Monaghan, on 21 October 1904. He was the fourth child of James and Bridget Kavanagh. Educated locally, he was a keen reader and was composing verse by his twelfth birthday.

Kavanagh's growing interest in literature and his own efforts at composition made him feel an outsider in the farming community around his home. After leaving school in 1916, he worked on his father's small farm and later as a cobbler. However, his abiding passion was poetry, and in September 1928 his poem, 'Freedom', won a prize in a competition sponsored by the *Irish Weekly Independent*. During the next ten months, fourteen of Kavanagh's poems appeared in this newspaper. The following autumn, he sent several poems to the *Irish Statesman*. Although they were rejected, he was advised to submit more material. Eventually, the *Irish Statesman* published three of his poems between 1929 and 1930. The editor, George Russell (AE), helped Patrick with practical advice on the craft of writing.

By 1930, the desire to move from the choking life of the small rural community had grown too powerful for Kavanagh to resist. He left for Dublin, the centre of literary life, and completed the journey on foot. Kavanagh was determined to make his mark in the world of literature.

In April 1936 his first book, *Ploughmen and Other Poems*, was published. Though well received in England and Dublin, it was ignored in Monaghan.

Kavanagh left for England to find both a publisher and a job with an English periodical. In 1938 his second book, *The Green Fool*, was published in London. Unfortunately the book's circulation was stopped by a lawsuit brought by Oliver St John Gogarty, who objected to a sketch in which Kavanagh claimed to have mistaken Gogarty's maid for his mistress. Damages of £100 were awarded against Kavanagh and the book became a bestseller.

On his return from England, Kavanagh moved between Dublin and Monaghan. He decided to leave the farm for good in 1939 and settle in Dublin, determined to earn his living by the pen. There, Kavanagh became involved with a literary group which met in the Palace Bar. Although part of this clique, he was a rough outsider who lacked the social graces of city society. He distrusted their commitment to literature, considering them to be critics rather than creators. In this environment, Kavanagh worked at his poetry, scraping a living in journalism. He wrote a social column for the *Irish Press* and film reviews for *The Standard*. Kavanagh turned his sharp attention to literature in a monthly column in *Envoy* entitled 'Diary'. He also contributed articles, short stories and poems to *The Bell*, *The Irish Times* and the *Dublin Magazine*. In 1942, Kavanagh's long poem, 'The Great Hunger', appeared.

When *Envoy* ceased publication, Kavanagh and his brother, Peter, began writing and publishing their own newspaper, *Kavanagh's Weekly*, in April 1952. This journal, bristling with controversy, appeared for only thirteen weeks. Following the publication of another collection of his poems in 1947, *A Soul for Sale*, the novel, *Tarry Flynn*, appeared in 1948.

In London after the close of *Kavanagh's Weekly*, Kavanagh felt that an article about him which appeared in *The Leader* was neither accurate nor fair. He brought a libel action against the paper. After lengthy legal proceedings, he agreed to a settlement.

In 1955 Kavanagh had a cancerous lung removed. He spent the summer of 1955 recuperating, much of it along the banks of the Grand Canal, which gave him new enthusiasm for writing again. A lecturing position in University College, Dublin, eased his financial position. 'Come Dance with Kitty Stobling' and other poems was published in 1960. *Self-Portrait* followed in 1962. In 1964, his *Collected Poems* was published, strengthening his reputation both inside and outside the country.

Kavanagh married Kathleen Maloney in April 1967, but died on the last day of November that same year. A novel, *By Night Understood*, was published posthumously in 1977.

Patrick and Kathleen Kavanagh on their wedding day

(1956-   )

John James Kelly was born in Carrick-on-Suir on 21 May 1956. He was known as Sean to avoid confusion with his father. The family owned a 48-acre farm in the townland of Carraghduff. He received his early education at Crehana National School and attended secondary school in Carrick-on-Suir, travelling the three-mile journey each morning and evening by bicycle.

Sean soon joined his eldest brother, Joe, as a member of the town's cycling club, Carrick Wheelers. In 1970, in his first competitive race, he sprinted past Joe and everyone else to win. Encouraged by his success, he set himself a stern schedule of training. During this period he worked as an apprentice bricklayer. Kelly's determination resulted in him taking the Irish Junior Championship in 1972. He also retained the title the following year. Kelly was equally successful in senior championships, which included an impressive victory on a stage of the Tour of Britain in 1975. His devastating sprinting power drew much attention.

Further encouraging results in France gave Kelly the necessary confidence to enter the professional circuit in 1977 with the Belgian-based Flandria team. He gained his first professional victories at Lugano and the Circuit de L'Indre, where he outsprinted the legendary Eddie Merckx to claim the winner's jersey. He increased his training routine and subjected himself to a specially controlled diet designed to maximise energy and strength. In 1978, during his first big Tour de France, he won a stage as a *domestique* (second-seeded cyclist on a team). In 1979 he won the Grand Prix de Cannes. During the 1980 Tour of Spain, when he was cycling for Splendos, Kelly had five stage wins to his credit, giving him points victory and fourth place overall. He also won two stages that year in the Tour de France. In 1982, now cycling in the Sem-France Loire colours, he took his first green jersey (best sprinter) as points winner of the Tour de France. He was the first cyclist from the English-speaking world to do so. He subsequently won the green jersey on two other occasions, becoming the only man in cycling history to achieve this. As leader of the Sem-

France Loire team in 1982, Kelly won his first Paris–Nice race and went on to take third place in the World Championships. The following season, he won his first one-day classic in Italy's Tour of Lombardy, and also the Tour of Switzerland despite a broken collar-bone. 1983 was the year in which he achieved another ambition, if only for a day—the yellow jersey in the Tour de France.

From 1984 to 1989, Kelly was ranked as No. 1 cyclist in the world, an astonishingly consistent achievement considering the fierce competition. His bravery in sprinting through gaps where other cyclists hesitated, his nerve and fierce competitiveness have made his name a legend in modern cycling. He was one of the first cyclists to break the French and Belgian domination in the sport.

Among thirty-three wins in 1984, Kelly won the Paris–Roubaix Classic, a notoriously taxing one-day 254 km race known as 'The Hell of the North'. There was also the Paris–Nice race, a competition in which he has been singularly successful over the years. He recorded his sixth consecutive win in that race in 1987, an unparalleled record in cycling history.

Kelly's strength and determination saw him achieve his highest position in the Tour de France in 1985, finishing fourth and collecting his third green jersey. In the same year he regained the Tour of Lombardy title and delighted his home country by winning Ireland's premier race, the Nissan Classic, a title which he retained the following year.

Though troubled by injury, Kelly still swept to victory in the 1988 Tour of Spain, cycling for the Spanish team KAS. Other victories such as the 1989 Liege–Bastogne–Liege Classic and the Tour of Switzerland followed. Recently, age, injury and family responsibilities (he is married with twins) have conspired to remove Kelly from his No. 1 ranking. In September 1991, however, his ever-strong determination saw him take the Nissan Classic once again. This was followed by victory in the Tour of Lombardy (October 1991). In 1992 he joined the Spanish team Lotus Festina.

After fifteen years in the saddle, riding more than 100 races each year and a lifetime of rigorous training have taken their toll on Sean Kelly. But among cyclists and supporters worldwide, he will always be one of cycling's greatest champions.

(1876-1947)

James Larkin was born in Liverpool, England, on 21 January 1876. His Irish parents were very poor and he spent his childhood with his grandparents in Newry, Co. Down. When James was only nine years old, he went back to Liverpool where he got a job which paid only 12½ pence per week. He worked as a seaman for a while and then went to work as a foreman on the Liverpool docks. When the workers went on strike, James sided with them and soon lost his job. Larkin believed that working people were being unfairly treated by their employers. So he spent much of his time working for the Union of Dock Labourers. Because he was such a wonderful speaker he encouraged many people to join him.

In 1907, Larkin moved to Belfast. There was trouble on the Belfast docks, and he quickly became a leader. He convinced the dockers not to handle certain goods—this was called 'blacking'. And he encouraged other Belfast workers to strike in sympathy with the dockers. The workers were glad to follow such a strong leader. But Larkin's union was worried that he was too aggressive. They thought he might do more harm than good. This did not please Larkin, so he moved to Dublin. His dream was to start a union for the workers that would help them fight for better conditions. In 1909, Larkin formed the Irish Transport and General Workers Union (ITGWU). Many unskilled workers joined him because they saw Larkin as their only hope. Up until then the employers made all the decisions about everything. The workers had no say in how long they worked or how much they were paid. They lived in terrible, crowded slums and often did not have enough money to feed their families, or to light a fire. So it was easy for a man like Larkin to get thousands of men to join his union. The employers soon became alarmed that one man was so powerful and popular with the poor workers of Dublin.

In 1913, the employers decided it was time to smash Larkin's union. The employers' leader was William Martin Murphy. He was the owner of both the daily newspaper, the *Irish Independent*, and Clery's department store. He was also director of the Dublin United Tramway Company. Murphy told his workers they would have to sign a pledge or promise to remain loyal to their employers. The workers were furious! With Larkin as their leader, they had the courage to go against Murphy. They refused to handle his newspaper and left the trams standing in the streets. Murphy acted quickly. He locked the workers out of their jobs. Many other employers soon followed his example. When the workers went out in sympathy, they too were locked out. Soon about 100,000 Dublin workers were unemployed.

The Great Dublin Lockout went on for eight months. During this time terrible hardships were suffered by the workers. Many were close to starvation. 'Big Jim' Larkin gave them courage through his powerful speeches. He got into trouble with the police for causing unrest. He even had to put on a disguise when he was delivering a speech at a workers' meeting in Sackville Street (now O'Connell Street). The police charged the crowd at this meeting and two people were killed. Larkin was sentenced to seven months in prison but was later set free.

The strike and lockout ended early in 1914. It had been a hard struggle, but the workers finally won the right to fair employment. In October 1914, Larkin decided that he would go to America to raise money for his union. But his strong ideas were not welcome in America and he ended up in prison again. He was released in 1923 and returned home to Ireland where he received a hero's welcome.

Back in Dublin Larkin found he was in trouble with his own union. He said the ITGWU was not working hard enough for workers' rights. The union disagreed, and in 1924 they expelled Larkin. But this did not stop Big Jim. With his brother Peter, he founded the Workers' Union of Ireland. He went on to become a Dáil deputy for a total of eight years. His last big success was to win a fortnight's annual holiday for manual workers following a fourteen-week strike.

Big Jim Larkin, the workers' friend, died in Dublin on 30 January 1947 and was buried in Glasnevin Cemetery. He left only £4.50. A statue by the sculptor Oisin Kelly showing Larkin now stands in College Green in Dublin.

A Dublin slum scene

(1899-1971)

Sean Lemass was born at Ballybrack, Co. Dublin, on 15 July 1899. His father, a draper in Capel Street, Dublin, was an active supporter of the Irish Parliamentary Party. Lemass received his education at the Christian Brothers O'Connell Schools.

Although he looked older, Lemass was only fifteen when he joined the Irish Volunteers. There he was placed under the captaincy of Éamon de Valera. During the Easter Rising in 1916, Lemass fought in the General Post Office. Because of his youth, he was released soon after the Rising, escaping deportation and returning to school. For a while he lay low, working in his father's drapery. Gradually, however, he returned to the Volunteers, rising steadily in the ranks to become a full-time officer. Playing an active role in the War of Independence (1919–21), he was arrested in December 1920 and sentenced to a year's internment at Ballykinlar, Co. Down.

Lemass was opposed to the terms of the 1921 Anglo-Irish Treaty which brought the War of Independence to an end. He was adjutant to the garrison commandant when anti-Treaty members of the Republican Army occupied the Four Courts in Dublin, signalling the start of the Civil War. After the besieged force inside the building surrendered, Lemass escaped. He was later captured and spent a year's captivity in the Curragh Camp and Mountjoy Jail until his release in December 1923. During his imprisonment, he became an enthusiastic reader of history and economics. Elected to the Dáil in 1925 as Sinn Féin member in Dublin, he did not take his seat. When the Fianna Fáil Party was formed in 1926, Lemass became its secretary. Under his management a highly efficient political party was built up. In 1932, de Valera appointed Lemass as Minister for Industry and Commerce in the first Fianna Fáil government. Except for brief interruptions during periods of opposition, he held this ministry until 1959. During World War II, he was also Minister for Supplies. In 1945, he became Tánaiste (Deputy Prime Minister).

During the 1930s, Lemass supported a policy of protective tariffs which helped him build up Irish industry. He set up large public companies such as Bord na Móna (established in order to develop the native peat industry), Aer Lingus, Ireland's national airline, and the country's first shipping company, Irish Shipping.

In 1959, Lemass succeeded de Valera as Taoiseach. During this period he pursued a vigorous policy of economic expansion. Foreign investment was encouraged. In 1965, he re-established free trade with Britain as a preparatory move towards joining the European Economic Community (EEC). His confident economic leadership created a mood of cultural and financial optimism, forcing an inward-looking society to develop new horizons.

In 1965, Lemass displayed characteristic courage in visiting the Prime Minister of Northern Ireland, Captain Terence O'Neill, in an effort to improve cross-border relations.

Resigning from the office of Taoiseach in 1966, Lemass left the Dáil in 1969. He died in Dublin on 11 May 1971.

(1865-1953)

Maud Gonne was born near Aldershot in England, probably on 20 December 1865. Her father, an army captain, was widowed in 1871 when Maud's mother died of tuberculosis. As a result, she and her younger sister were educated by a governess on the French Riviera. Her father rose to the rank of colonel in the British Army and was posted to Dublin Castle in 1882. Maud, already a striking beauty, was his hostess until his death of fever four years later.

Following this loss, Maud lived for a while in London. However, because of ill health, she was sent to recover at Royat in the French Auvergne. There she met and fell in love with Lucien Millevoye, a politician and journalist. They pledged to commit themselves to the cause of Irish independence and the recovery of the French area of Alsace-Lorraine from Germany.

Returning to Ireland, Maud plunged into the protest against evictions in Donegal. Despite being English, she also campaigned for and helped to secure the release of Irish political prisoners from Portland Jail. When she went back to France in 1890, she resumed her relationship with Millevoye. The couple had two children, but only their daughter, Iseult, survived. Maud and Lucien parted when she found out that his interest in Irish independence was false.

During the next few years, Maud Gonne committed herself to a variety of nationalist activities, dividing her life between Ireland, Britain, France, America and Scotland. With the poet, William Butler Yeats, whose marriage proposal she had rejected in 1891 (Yeats dedicated many of his poems to her), she founded an Irish society in Paris. She was a member of the secret Irish Republican Brotherhood (IRB). She founded her own revolutionary society for women, Inghinidhe na nÉireann (Daughters of Ireland), in 1900. She had earlier published a news-sheet in Paris, hoping to attract French support for Irish independence.

Maud Gonne was a tireless spokesperson for the nationalist movement, always busy organising meetings and fundraising events. In July 1900, Inghinidhe na hÉireann arranged a huge party for Dublin children as a method of distracting public attention from the official welcoming ceremonies for Queen Victoria's visit. She was also actively involved in opposing British recruitment for the Boer War.

In 1902, Maud Gonne took the title role in Yeats's *Cathleen Ní Houlihan*, representing Ireland's struggle for independence. Her beauty and the strength of her acting received widespread acclaim.

After becoming a convert to Catholicism, she married Major John MacBride who had fought in an Irish brigade in the Boer War. They had one son, Seán, but their marriage collapsed within two years. Major MacBride returned to Ireland where he was executed after the Easter Rebellion in 1916. Maud spent the next few months in Paris, returning to Dublin in 1917. She was interned the following year in Holloway Jail, London, for six months. On her release, she worked with the White Cross, organising relief during the War of Independence for the victims of violence and their families. Supporting the anti-Treaty side during the Civil War, she formed the Women's Prisoners' Defence League to assist Republican prisoners and their families. She was imprisoned once again in 1923, but was released when she embarked on a hunger strike.

In 1938, Maud Gonne MacBride published the story of her earlier life, *A Servant of the Queen*. She died on 27 April 1953 at Roebuck House, Clonskeagh, Dublin, where she had lived since 1922. She was buried in the Republican plot in Glasnevin Cemetery, Dublin.

(1904-1988)

Sean MacBride was born in Paris on 26 January 1904, the son of revolutionary parents. His father, John, was executed after the 1916 Easter Rising, and his mother was the famous Maud Gonne. Sean's early schooling was at St Louis de Gonzaga College in Paris. Later, he went to Mount St Benedict's, Gorey, University College, Dublin, and finally the King's Inns.

Considering the nationalist ideas of his parents, it is perhaps not surprising that MacBride joined the Irish Volunteers. He saw active service during the War of Independence (1919–21) and was attached to the General Headquarters Staff under Michael Collins. In the subsequent Treaty negotiations in London, he acted as personal aide to Collins. Opposing the Treaty, he was imprisoned in the Civil War, but was later released. He also opposed the policies of the fledgling Fianna Fáil government in the early 1930s. MacBride was made Chief of Staff of the Irish Republican Army (IRA) in 1936, having lived for periods in Paris and London working as a journalist.

MacBride was called to the bar in 1937. In that same year he resigned from the IRA. He declared that, owing to changed constitutional circumstances, it was possible to further nationalistic causes in Ireland by political means rather than through armed struggle. As a barrister, he defended former colleagues in the Republican movement with great skill.

MacBride founded the political party, Clann na Poblachta, in 1946. It was a partner in the coalition government from 1946 to 1951, with MacBride as Minister for External Affairs. He had been elected as a Dáil deputy for Co. Dublin in 1947. MacBride's voice was a strong one in coalition. He successfully campaigned against Irish membership of NATO, thereby emphasising Irish neutrality.

The ending of his political career saw no let up in his energetic schedule. He then concentrated on international issues such as human rights and worldwide peace initiatives. MacBride was a founder-member of Amnesty International, an organisation which sought the release of prisoners of conscience and opposed torture and execution. He was international chairman of Amnesty from 1961 to 1974. Between 1963 and 1971, he was Secretary General of the International Commission of Jurists which examined the worldwide state of human rights. His many other distinguished and varied portfolios included: Chairman, Special Committee of International Non-Government Organisation on Human Rights (1968–74); Chairman, International Peace Bureau, Geneva, 1969 (President, 1974); Chairman of UNESCO International Commission on Communication Problems; and President, Irish Campaign for Nuclear Disarmament. He was honoured with the Nobel Peace Prize in 1974 and the Lenin Peace Prize in 1977, the first person ever to be awarded both. In 1980, he was granted the UNESCO Silver Medal.

Sean MacBride attempted to persuade US firms in the North of Ireland to follow the MacBride Principles, an attempt to establish fair employment practices for Catholics. This won widespread support although many northern nationalist leaders like John Hume opposed the MacBride Principles, believing that they did more harm than good.

On 15 January 1988, Sean MacBride, revolutionary and man of peace, died at Roebuck House in Clonskeagh, Dublin. He was buried in the Republican plot, Glasnevin Cemetery. His life was a remarkable campaign for human rights.

(1884-1945)

John Francis McCormack was born in the midland town of Athlone, Co. Westmeath, on 14 June 1884. He was the fourth of eleven children. Educated by the Marist Brothers, he was clever at school and at the age of twelve won a scholarship to Summerhill College, Sligo. There he joined the choir where his clear voice soon earned him the role of soloist. Even at this early stage, however, a shadow of nervous fear troubled him before singing in public. This worry was to haunt him before every performance of his life. What if he opened his mouth and no sound came?

The highlight of McCormack's years at Summerhill was a concert in Sligo for which he received his first fee—five shillings.

At the height of his career, he would be paid at least £1,000 for a single performance.

When his schooling was over, McCormack joined St Peter's Church choir in Athlone. He received training and guidance from the local organist, Michael Kilkelly, who believed that his student's voice had enormous potential. Kilkelly sent him to Dublin to train with Vincent O'Brien, the foremost singing teacher in Ireland, who accepted McCormack into his choir. O'Brien worked at developing McCormack's voice. The young man worked hard, whether with the choir in practice, in concerts, or singing solo at private parties around the city.

After winning the Gold Medal at the 1902 Feis Cheoil (Ireland's annual musical competition), offers to sing at concerts began to arrive from all over the country. A short tour in America followed in 1903, during which McCormack became engaged to Lily Foley, an Irish soprano. He returned to London where he heard the great singer, Enrico Caruso, whose voice left him in awe and gave him an ambition to achieve a similar standard himself one day. To do this, McCormack realised that he needed to study in Italy, the home of opera. By saving hard and through the generosity of friends, he eventually trained in Italy under the maestro, Sabatini, perfecting his scale work and breathing techniques. Late in 1905, Sabatini managed to secure a part for John McCormack in *Amico Fritz* at the little seaport town of Savona. Because the Italians could not pronounce his name, and because opera singers at that time were expected to have Italian names, he appeared under the name Giovanni Foli (chosen in honour of his fianceé, Lily, whom he married that July). In 1907, at the age of twenty-three, McCormack made his début in *Cavalleria Rusticana* at Covent Garden in London, the youngest tenor ever to sing a principal role there. In 1909, he appeared at the Manhattan Opera House, New York, in *La Traviata*. His success continued and in 1911 McCormack toured Australia. He sang sixty-seven concerts between November 1912 and May 1913, travelling across America. At one concert in New York, 7,000 people packed into the hall and 5,000 more were turned away.

McCormack now turned his attention from opera to the concert stage. There, his success and popularity was extraordinary. He was a masterly singer of the lyric. The most popular song associated with him, 'I Hear You Calling Me', became a bestseller. Of the hundreds of records he made, this song earned him more money than any other. At the peak of his career he earned more than £200,000 a year.

McCormack was a very disciplined singer and was never known to be late for a performance. He had a magnetic personality, loved company and spent lavishly. In 1928, Pope Pius IX, whom McCormack admired, created him a Papal Count for his fundraising on behalf of Church charities. In 1932 he was given the honour of singing at the Eucharistic Congress in Dublin's Phoenix Park before one million people. He was accompanied by a choir of 500 men and boys which was conducted by his old teacher, Dr O'Brien.

John McCormack died in his house at Booterstown, Co. Dublin, on 16 September 1945, the strain of his remarkable breathing during his singing years having weakened his lungs and heart. He is remembered in America as a legend, in Britain and other countries as the greatest lyric tenor of the century, and in Ireland as its most famous singer.

JOHN McCORMACK

(1961-)

Barry McGuigan was born in Clones, Co. Monaghan, on 28 February 1961. His father, Pat McGuigan, was a well-known showband singer during the 1960s (he had come third in the 1968 Eurovision Song Contest). Pat himself had had ambitions to be an amateur boxer and fought under the name Patsy McGeehan. His two eldest sons, Dermot and Barry, began to share this enthusiasm at an early age, going with their father to local amateur fights. Barry first joined Wattle-bridge Club across the border in Fermanagh for a short time and then Smithboro Club, a few miles outside Clones. His dedication and aggression marked him apart from the other young hopefuls. His coach, Danny McEntee, worked hard to help the youngster make the

best of his power. Barry was soon winning local competitions and the 'Clones Cyclone' took the Golden Shamrock Juvenile title at the age of thirteen before adding the national under-fourteen championship to his belt.

In the year he left school, Barry won the Juvenile title, displaying a vicious hook. He worked at his left-hand punch, trained for hours on the punch bag and watched videos of professional boxers to learn techniques and moves. In 1976, Barry beat Phil Sutcliff (later a senior champion), and a year later he became the youngest ever Ulster Senior Champion. In 1978, he won the national bantamweight final and a gold medal at the 1978 Commonwealth Games in Edmonton, Canada. In the 1980 Moscow Olympic Games, he lost on points in the second series of matches. Bouncing back from this setback, Barry decided to turn professional in 1981. Barney Eastwood, a wealthy business-man and boxing promoter, became his manager. Barry's new trainer was Eddie Shaw, an experienced fighter. Barry's profes-sional career started well, with four knock-outs in his first six fights, although a defeat in his bout against Peter Eubanks prevented him from attaining an unbeaten record. In December 1981 he married Sandra Mealiff, a local girl whom he had known for many years. The couple now have four children.

Eight victories in eight contests in 1982 pushed Barry into the British and European top-ten boxers in the feather-weight class. However, one fight on 12 June 1982 in which he defeated a young Nigerian, Asymin Mustapha, was to remain a painful memory. Because of his injuries in that fight, Mustapha was put on a life-support machine. Barry heard the news of his opponent's death in December. He was deeply shocked and seriously considered retiring. But he returned to the ring and his path over the next two years was strewn with victories. These included the British featherweight title, and the European title (November 1983) which were fought before rapturous crowds in Belfast's King's Hall.

By this time, Barry's success and personality had united Irish people, north and south, Protestant and Catholic, in their support, and seemed to be advancing the cause of peace. Following his win and successful defence of his European title in March 1985, Barry was at last in line for a world title match against the world champion, Eusebio Pedroza from Panama. On 8 June 1985, Ireland came to a halt to see Barry fight for a world title. McGuigan relentlessly hounded the tiring champion and won the World Featherweight title after an exciting fifteen rounds.

In the searing heat of Las Vegas, in June 1986, he lost his title in a sensational bout with the little-fancied Steve Cruz. Barry was frustrated by this defeat, as well as with the problems which were growing between himself and Eastwood. Barry and Eastwood soon separated amid legal proceedings. Following a defeat in June 1988, Barry McGuigan retired from the ring. Since then he has embarked on a series of personal appearances, commentary work on fights and has furthered his interest in rally driving.

BARRY McGUIGAN

(1923-1986)

Siobhán McKenna was born on 24 May 1923 in Belfast. Her parents were Owen McKenna, a lecturer in mathematical physics at Queen's University, Belfast, and Margaret O'Reilly, a designer. The young child spoke only Irish at home until she went to school. When she was five, the family moved to Galway where her father became Professor of Mathematics at University College, Galway.

After a period at Galway's Dominican Convent School, Siobhán was educated at St Louis Convent School in Monaghan and succeeded in winning a scholarship to Galway University. She was an all-round high achiever and her father had strong hopes of her following in his footsteps. However, her real interest lay in the arts so she studied English, French and Irish literature. Receiving a first class honours degree, she was offered a scholarship in French literature for a year's study in Paris. But the Abbey Theatre, then at the peak of its fame, offered her an audition and she decided to join, having had earlier acting experience in Galway's Irish language theatre, the Taibhdhearc. There she appeared in Shakespearian roles and in plays by O'Casey and O'Neill. Her talent also found expression in writing and she was the author of short stories both in English and Irish. At the Abbey she met Denis O'Dea and they were married in 1946.

Siobhán made her London début in 1947. Successful performances included Regina in *Ghosts*, Pegeen Mike in *The Playboy of the Western World* (a role she was to make her own), and the title role in *Heloise*. In 1954, in George Bernard Shaw's *St Joan*, she held audiences spellbound from the moment she appeared on stage. It was to be her own favourite role.

Following her successful American début in 1955, Siobhán remained there for some time, where she included the role of Hamlet in her repertoire. In 1960, she returned to Europe, touring with *The Playboy of the Western World*. Apart from stage performances, she was also successful in several films, including *King of Kings*, *Of Human Bondage*, *Doctor Zhivago*, *Philadelphia, Here I Come* and the screen version of *The Playboy of the Western World*.

Despite the lure of travel and international success, Siobhán McKenna always returned to Ireland, her theatrical and domestic home. In Dublin in 1966, she created another memorable role, that of Juno in O'Casey's *Juno and the Paycock*. A highlight of her later career was the one-woman show, *Here Are Ladies*. It was staged in 1970 and was an anthology of women as seen by Irish writers, including the Molly Bloom soliloquy. A sparkling portrait of the famous actress Sarah Bernhardt followed in 1977. Her last role was Mammo in *Bailegangaire* by Tom Murphy.

In 1975, Siobhán McKenna was appointed to the Irish Council of State. She died of a heart attack following surgery for lung cancer in Dublin on 16 September 1986 and is buried in Rahoon Cemetery, Galway.

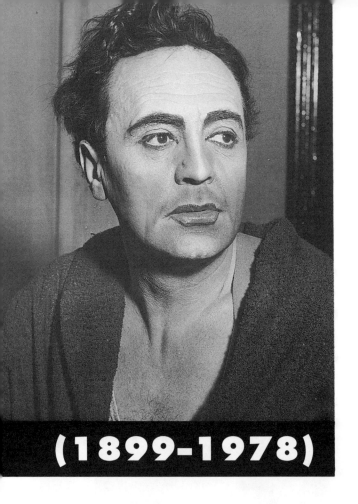

(1899-1978)

Michael Alfred Willmore (Mícheál Mac Liammóir) was born in London on 25 October 1899. In 1911 he became a child actor in the city's West End Little Theatre where he appeared with Noel Coward In *Peter Pan*. From 1915 to 1916, he studied at the Slade School of Art. After spending seven years painting on the Continent, he came to Ireland in 1927 to join his brother-in-law Anew McMaster's touring company. The group travelled from town to town, performing Shakespeare under oil lamps on makeshift stages. It was during this period that he met the English actor, Hilton Edwards, his lifelong personal and professional partner.

During his early years in London, Michael had joined the Gaelic League. He became a fluent Irish speaker and changed his name to its Irish version. He was one of the founders of Galway's Irish Theatre, Taibhdhearc na Gaillimhe, which opened with a performance of his *Diarmaid agus Gráinne* on 27 August 1928. As well as playing the leading role, Mac Liammóir designed and painted the sets. Two months later, he and Edwards founded the Gate Theatre in Dublin. They opened with Ibsen's *Peer Gynt* in the premises now called the Peacock Theatre. In 1930, Mac Liammóir and Edwards moved to the present Gate Theatre. The Abbey's dramatic standards had, at this time, been lowered by producing tame 'kitchen comedy'. So the Gate established a high level of artistic excellence and excitement (and at times, controversy), staging a wide range of international dramas. The Gate company toured England, America, Greece, Malta and Egypt. The theatre had the good fortune to be generously supported by the patronage of the sixth Earl of Longford who formed a separate company, the Longford Players, in 1936. Both companies shared the theatre.

Mac Liammóir's influence was evident everywhere in the Gate. He acted, directed, wrote, translated and designed. Soon he gained an international reputation, particularly in Shakespearian roles. In 1932, on tour in Denmark, he was awarded the Kronberg Gold Medal for his role in *Hamlet* at the Theatre Festival in Helsingor (Elsinore of the play). He also played Hamlet in New York to great acclaim. His writing was equally productive, with plays and poetry in both English and Irish.

After starring in *Ill Met by Moonlight* in London, he made his New York début in 1948 in *John Bull's Other Island*. The following year Mac Liammóir starred as Iago in Orson Welles' film, *Othello*. Welles had himself begun his career at the Gate.

Mac Liammóir's most successful production came at the age of sixty in 1960 with his classic, *The Importance of Being Oscar*. This one-man show was immensely popular, with Mac Liammóir's stylish charm creating a marvellous portrait of Oscar Wilde. His final performance as Oscar (his 1384th) took place at the

Gate in 1975. Earlier, in 1963, his second one-man show, *I Must Be Talking to my Friends*, was staged. It was followed by a third such show two years later, *Talking about Yeats*. In 1973 he had been granted the Freedom of Dublin.

Despite failing eyesight and suffering a stroke, Mac Liammóir's theatrical manner and witty conversational powers stayed with him until his death in Dublin on 6 March 1978. Mac Liammóir was one of Ireland's greatest twentieth-century actors, whose roles ranged from the lightest romantic comedy to dark tragedy. He is buried in St Fintan's Cemetery, Sutton, Co. Dublin.

MÍCHEÁL MAC LIAMMÓIR

(1110-1171)

Diarmuid MacMurrough was born at Ferns, Co. Wexford, in A.D. 1110. He was the third son of the King of Leinster. Bordered by ocean, river and mountain, the Mac-Murrough territory lay close to the busy shipping routes to Europe.

Twelfth-century Ireland was ruled by a high king. Under him were lesser kings who collected taxes for local clans. There were many battles over land and cattle. However, the Brehon Laws attempted to deal with such crimes.

As a child Diarmuid was fostered, living with another family. Fosterage was common at the time because it strength-ened friendship and loyalty between the clans. Diarmuid enjoyed himself, learning chess, swimming and horse-riding. His father was poisoned by Dublin Vikings and buried with a dog as an insult. After his two brothers died, Diarmuid was elected King at the age of sixteen, despite the Brehon Law that a king had to be eighteen. Diarmuid's first conquest was a convent in Kildare, where he killed many and replaced the abbess with a woman of his own choice. He then captured the Viking city of Waterford. He tackled problems inside his kingdom by crushing a rebellion in 1140 after blinding seventeen hostages. Diarmuid's ruthless action brought peace.

Diarmuid married and lived in Ferns. He loved his three children and never fos-tered them, teaching them himself as well as hiring a tutor.

Diarmuid's lifelong enemy was Tier-nan O'Rourke. O'Rourke vowed revenge when his wife, Dervogilla, was kidnapped by Diarmuid. In 1156 a fire destroyed Ferns. While Diarmuid's men were rebuilding, the armies of O'Rourke and the High King, O'Connor, advanced on Wexford. Diarmuid watched as neighbouring chieftains joined the invaders. He burned his own castle to stop his enemies resting there, but was defeated in battle.

He hoped to raise an army to recover his lost kingdom. Henry allowed Diarmuid to recruit an army in Wales. Among those he chose was Strongbow (Richard le Clare). Diarmuid offered him his daughter Aoife in marriage and the throne of Leinster on his death if Strongbow would come to his assis-tance. Other Norman leaders, Fitzstephen and Fitzgerald, also offered their assistance.

In May 1169, 500 Normans under Fitzstephen landed on Bannow Strand, Wexford. The town surrendered after the defenders' ships were burned. Diarmuid's support grew as chieftains returned behind his banner. Soon Leinster was his again. But Diarmuid wanted to be High King. Strongbow sent over another army and arrived later himself. Wexford was taken when the Normans broke through the city walls. Amid the destruction Strongbow married Diarmuid's daughter, Aoife.

Diarmuid soon controlled most of Ireland. The High King was worried. He had one trump card—Diarmuid's favourite son, Conor, whom he held as a hostage. O'Rourke urged the King to kill the boy and Conor was hacked to death. This shocking blow was too much for Diarmuid. He had gambled with his son's life and lost. With all his plans shattered, he returned home where he died, a broken-hearted old man, in 1171.

(1868-1927)

Constance Gore-Booth was born in London on 4 February 1868, the eldest child of the family. Her father, Henry Gore-Booth, was an Arctic explorer and a landlord in the west of Ireland. As a child, Constance went to the lovely Lissadell estate in Co. Sligo. During one of her visits, she was distressed to see tenants being evicted from their homes, too poor to pay their rent. Later she became involved in supplying food to hungry tenants.

Constance lived the pleasurable life of a young lady in fashionable London during autumn and winter each year, but the visit of William Butler Yeats to Lissadell in 1894 was a turning point. Listening to his stories of Irish myths and folklore and his passionate political ideas, she was stirred into activity. At that time, women were not allowed to vote in elections or to become Members of Parliament. Constance decided to join the suffragettes who were fighting for women's rights, including the right to vote.

In 1893, Constance studied art in London and later travelled to Paris, hoping to become a painter. There she met and married Count Casimir Dunin-Markievicz, also an artist, who had a large estate in Poland. After travelling abroad, they returned to Sligo where their daughter Maeve was born. In 1903 they settled in Dublin. Ireland's capital was an exciting city at that time, a centre for artists, actors, writers and politicians. Constance took part in Sinn Féin meetings and parades and in 1909 she founded Na Fianna Éireann in which boys were trained in the use of weaponry.

Constance was arrested in 1911 for her revolutionary activities and questioned before being released. It was the first of many times that the Countess would find herself behind bars. During the Dublin workers' strike in 1913 and the harsh winter lock-out that followed, she organised a food kitchen in Liberty Hall to feed starving strikers. Constance then joined the Irish Citizens Army. During the 1916 Rising, she was among those who occupied the College of Surgeons at St Stephen's Green. Although condemned to death when the rebellion was crushed, her sentence was commuted to life imprisonment and she was transported to England.

Under the general amnesty of 1917, Countess Markievicz was released and immediately became a convert to Catholicism. Shortly after, with many other Sinn Féin leaders, she was imprisoned again in

England. She was elected for Sinn Féin in Dublin—the first woman ever to be elected to the British parliament. However, as Sinn Féin believed in Irish self-government, she refused to accept her seat in London. Sinn Féin won a majority in the 1918 general election and decided to set up an independent government in Dublin. In the first Dáil, Constance was made Secretary for Labour. However, the British government, which claimed to rule Ireland, opposed Irish government and she was imprisoned again.

Under the Treaty which ended the War of Independence, Constance was released. Standing against the Treaty, she fought on the Republican side during the Civil War. Constance later toured America to harvest support for the anti-Treaty side. Although growing old, she was imprisoned again in 1923 and went on hunger strike for a while. She joined Fianna Fáil (formed by de Valera in 1926) and was elected to the Dáil again in 1927. Her husband, Count Casimir, came from Poland to be with her when she died later that year on 15 July. Countess Markievicz was buried at Glasnevin Cemetery, Dublin.

Countess Markievicz arriving with fellow TD Joseph McGuinness for a session of the Dáil in 1921

(1892-1975)

Marie Helena Martin was born in Glenageary, Co. Dublin, on 25 April 1892. She was the eldest of twelve children. Her father was a wealthy Dublin businessman who dealt in timber. She had a privileged childhood, with a German governess living with the family in their large house, frequent holidays and parties. She contacted rheumatic fever in 1904, a sickness which was to leave her a legacy of ill health throughout her life. On St Patrick's Day 1907, tragedy struck when her father accidentally killed himself with a revolver.

In 1908, having attended school in Leeson Street, Marie was sent to a convent in Harrogate, Yorkshire. Her mother hoped the local spa waters might improve Marie's health. Later, she was sent to a finishing school in Bonn, Germany. Home again in 1910, she began to become involved in charitable work, visiting the sick and poor in her neighbourhood.

With the onset of World War I, Marie trained as a nurse in the Richmond Hospital and was called for service in Malta, treating the wounded of Gallipoli. It was exhausting work but she accepted the hard discipline without complaint. She later served in France and also worked in a hospital for wounded officers in Leeds. Her experiences convinced her that medical work had immense potential for spiritual as well as physical healing.

In January 1921, after being approached by Bishop Shanahan, an African missionary, Marie left with Agnes Ryan for Calabar, Nigeria, to take charge of a boarding school. There she saw the need for an organisation of women which would combine missionary work with medical expertise. Returning to Ireland in 1923, she was plagued by pleurisy, heart trouble, appendicitis and other ailments. But her determination to establish a religious order involved in medical work never faltered. This was despite the fact that, under existing Church rules, women religious were prohibited from practising medicine. Eventually, her case was considered, and in 1934 she was appointed matron of a Benedictine school at Glenstal, Co. Limerick. Her breakthrough finally came in 1936 when Pope Pius XI gave permission to women religious to perform medical work. In 1937, she founded the Medical Missionaries of Mary in southern Nigeria.

Marie, now Mother Mary, took extreme care in drafting the constitution by which her nuns would live. Under her organisation, a house for students was established at Booterstown, Co. Dublin, a novitiate opened at Callan, Co. Louth, and in 1939 a maternity hospital was built in Drogheda. The influential Cardinal Cushing became her lifelong friend and a generous patron. From 1937 to 1954, a surge of vocations increased the sisterhood from three to almost 300.

The work record of the Medical Missionaries of Mary was outstanding. In 1953 alone they treated over half a million cases of leprosy, malaria and other tropical diseases in twenty hospitals and clinics throughout Africa. Infant and maternal mortality decreased. Their mobile units tended patients in remote areas and a hundred African girls attended their nurse training schools.

By 1954 the Medical Missionaries had expanded to twenty-one houses. Mary Martin was at the centre of every development. In 1963, she received the Florence Nightingale Medal from the International Red Cross. In 1966 she became the first woman to receive the Freedom of Drogheda.

Following several years as an invalid, Mother Mary Martin died in her hospital in Drogheda on 27 January 1975 after a life of contemplation and activity, serving people of all races, creeds and classes.

Mother Mary Martin in Drogheda in 1967 with Cardinal Cody of Chicago and Cardinal Conway of Armagh

(1938-   )

Paddy Moloney was born on 1 August 1938 in Donnycarney, Dublin. His family was steeped in the lilt of traditional music. Paddy's earliest instrument was a plastic whistle which he taught himself to play at six years of age.

The youngster attended the Christian Brothers (Scoil Mhuire) in nearby Marino where he learned to play the piano and ukelele. Before long he realised that his musical preference was for the uilleann pipes, and he enrolled for weekly lessons with the well-known piper Leo Rowsome at the School of Music. At eleven years of age, Paddy won the under-14 piping section of the Dublin Feis. After the foundation of Comhaltas Ceolteoiri Eireann in 1951, Paddy went on to win All-Ireland medals.

In 1959, Paddy met whistle player, Sean Potts. Right from their first meeting the musical chemistry between the two was special. Sean and Paddy experimented and improvised, bouncing musical ideas off each other. By this time, Paddy was very busy playing in a quartet, in two ceili bands and in a group called the Three Squares. To earn a living he worked in the accounting department of Baxendales (builders' providers).

Paddy soon became a member of Seán Ó Riada's Ceoltóirí Cualann, playing pipes and whistle. Ó Riada saw his group as a folk ensemble which was ready to tackle arrangements, harmony and improvisation in a traditional medium. They first went public at the Abbey Theatre with Bryan Macmahon's play, *The Golden Folk*. By the mid-1960s, Ceoltóirí Cualann were known throughout the country, playing a series of radio programmes. However, by the end of the decade Ó Riada disbanded the group, to Paddy's disappointment.

Meanwhile, back in 1963, Garech de Brun, who had founded Claddagh Records, invited Paddy (just married to Rita O'Reilly) to assemble a group for an album. Paddy chose Michael Tubridy, Sean Potts, Martin Fay and Davey Fallon. They called themselves the Chieftains. The name came from a book title by John Montague, poet and a Director of Claddagh. Their first album was very well received. Concert engagements and media appearances further boosted the group's popularity, and their first TV programme was on Ulster Television in 1965. They became equally popular in England and Scotland.

In 1968, Paddy resigned from Baxendales to become manager of Claddagh Records. In the same year, the Chieftains attended the Edinburgh Festival. In 1970, the band received a rapturous reception at a concert in Dublin's National Stadium. Orchestral harper, Derek Bell, joined the group, adding a special dimension that Paddy felt had been missing up to then.

Following a sell-out concert at London's Albert Hall in 1975, the Chieftains became a professional group. Turning full-time meant a gruelling schedule, including a concert tour of Britain. In April 1976, the group won an Oscar with their music for the film, *Barry Lyndon*. In 1978, Paddy was asked by Joan Denise Moriarty, Director of the National Ballet Company, to provide a score for the ballet version of *The Playboy of the Western World*. The ballet was produced as part of that year's Dublin Theatre Festival and later televised by RTE.

The Chieftains broke all records when they played before their biggest ever audience—1¼ million people in the Phoenix Park, Dublin, on 29 September 1979, to celebrate the visit of Pope John Paul II to Ireland. They also performed the first public concert to be held in the National Concert Hall, Dublin. The following year they teamed up with a Chinese ensemble of musicians, dancers and singers in an exciting fusion of musical cultures. In April 1983, the Chieftains travelled to China on a unique tour. Among other venues, they actually played on the Great Wall of China. To mark the occasion, Paddy prepared an arrangement called, suitably, 'Off the Great Wall'. They made further musical history when they became the first group to give a concert in the Capital Building, Washington DC, USA.

In January 1984, the Chieftains were joined by the Milwaukee Symphony Orchestra to play their music from the successful TV series, 'The Year of the French'. 1984 was the group's twenty-first anniversary and after two sell-out tours of North America, they were awarded a gold disc.

The Chieftains performed the score for 'The Ballad of the Irish Horse' (composed by Paddy) which was screened in the United States. In 1987, the group released an album entitled 'James Galway and the Chieftains in Ireland'. They appeared with the great flautist in a series of concerts.

Trinity College, Dublin, conferred a Doctorate of Music on Paddy in recognition of his contribution to Irish music. He has played alongside many musical personalities: Paul McCartney, Mick Jagger, Eric Clapton, Van Morrison and Stevie Wonder. However, despite his personal successes, Paddy's priority is, as always, to play with the Chieftains, the greatest exponents of traditional Irish music.

(1779-1852)

Thomas Moore was born on 28 May 1779 at 12 Aungier Street, Dublin. He was the eldest son of a grocer and wine merchant. Moore attended Samuel Whyte's school and by eleven years of age was already taking part in amateur theatricals. His first poem was published when he was fifteen. By then, he had already taught himself to play the piano. In 1794, he went to Trinity College which had opened its doors to Catholics a year before. There he made friends with Robert Emmet who was one of the brightest debaters in the Historical Society. However, Moore had little sympathy for the activities of Emmet and his United Irishmen. Moore was also a companion of another Irishman, Edward Hudson, who gave him an interest in traditional Irish music. Although much of his time was spent debating, writing poetry and socialising, Moore studied hard and graduated in 1798. Encouraged by the Provost of TCD, he published a translation of Greek odes in 1800.

In 1799, Moore travelled to London to study law at the Middle Temple, but spent much time writing verse and enjoying the city's social life. At parties he was invited to sing his songs to his own piano accompaniment. In 1801, under the pen-name Thomas Little, he published a book of poems, *Poetical Works of the late Thomas Little Esquire*. In 1803, it was suggested that he might be Poet Laureate for Ireland, but he refused, since he feared that the position would demand his support for British government policy in Ireland.

Also in 1803, Moore was made registrar of the Admiralty Prize Court in Bermuda, but quiet island life was not for him. He travelled to the United States and Canada on his return journey, arriving back in London in 1804.

1806 saw the publication of *Epistles, Odes and Other Poems* which was criticised as immoral by the *Edinburgh Review*. Moore was so annoyed that he challenged the *Review*'s editor to a duel. Luckily, police interrupted the occasion, and, in time, Moore and the paper's editor became good friends.

Back in Dublin the following year, Moore's fame reached new heights. The publisher, William Power, suggested that he write verse to fit traditional Irish tunes, with musical arrangements by Sir John Stevenson. So began his *Melodies*, the work for which he became famous. The first volume appeared in 1807, the tenth in 1834. Some of the poems have become so well known that it might seem as if they are all traditional themselves. They include 'The Harp that once through Tara's Halls', 'The Meeting of the Waters' and 'The Last Rose of Summer'. The *Melodies* were very successful, earning Moore a lot of money and the name of Ireland's national lyric poet.

In 1808, Moore took up dramatics, acting at Richard Power's theatre in Kilkenny. Here he met a young actress, Bessie Pyke, who became his wife. They went to England in December 1810 where his long Eastern oriental poem *Lalla Rookh* was written for an advance of £3,000. In 1818, after it was revealed that his deputy in Bermuda had stolen £6,000, Moore went into hiding abroad for three years to avoid imprisonment. In 1822 he returned to his home in Wiltshire.

Moore's later years were occupied with the prose piece *The Fudge Family in Paris* (1818) and an unexceptional *History of Ireland* (1827). In 1832 he was asked to stand for parliament in Limerick and for the Dublin University, but he declined the offers. With his children all dead before him, Moore's last years were heavy with sadness. He died on 25 February 1852 and was buried in the little village of Sloperton, Wiltshire, where he had lived for many years.

THOMAS MOORE

(1945-   )

George Ivan Morrison was born in Belfast on 31 August 1945. He was the only son of a musical family, his mother being a respected jazz singer. He was brought up as a Jehovah's Witness. While attending Orangefield Secondary School, he took music lessons, mastering guitar, harmonica and saxophone by his thirteenth birthday. American jazz, country and blues were the main musical influences on the youngster through his father's huge record collection. At the age of fourteen he left school to play in a local showband, the Monarchs. Morrison, who sang and played saxophone, introduced rhythm and blues into their repertoire. The band later moved to London, playing in jazz circles where Van's love of the blues deepened. After a year, however, the group disbanded.

Van was forced then to support himself with manual work. In 1963 he met a young guitar player, Bill Harrison. The legendary group, Them, was born. Its highly controlled blues sound was complemented by Morrison's husky nasal tone. The group attracted a devoted regular audience at Belfast's Maritime Hotel. Philip Solomon signed them for Decca Records. In 1964, the single, 'Baby Please Don't Go', raced up the UK charts to No. 6. In April 1965, another single, 'Here Comes the Night', reached No. 2. After three very successful years, the band broke up during their 1966 tour of America. Van then returned to Belfast.

After a quiet period, Warner Brothers signed up Morrison, allowing him the creative freedom he had not enjoyed before. This resulted in a classic album, 'Astral Weeks' (1968), a milestone in popular music. Van's next album, 'Moondance' (1969), produced by himself, was a commercial success.

At this stage, Van was living with his wife Janet in America. He spent much of this period doing both concert tours and impromptu gigs. He also built his own studio and set up Caledonia Productions Company to become independent of the cut-throat side of the music business. His marriage to Janet broke up. The unhappiness of this is reflected in his 1972 album, 'St Dominic's Preview', a collection of songs heavy with emotion. Morrison was now tapping a rich creative seam, and within a year came 'Hard Nose The Highway', with hardhitting songs of love, deceit, history and nature. With his musicians he now plunged into a whirl of live performances throughout America and Europe, playing to huge audiences of devoted fans. A resultant live double album, 'Its Too Late To Stop Now' (1974), illustrated the power and poise of the concerts charting the highlights of Van Morrison's career up to then. The record was a landmark in live recording.

After a brief holiday in Ireland he returned to America to record a moody, romantic album, 'Veedon Fleece'. Over a period he built up a reputation as a difficult and moody man with little time for interviews and television appearances. Morrison's musical energies were now finding their most complete expression in jazz. After concerts in Europe and a successful US tour, little was heard or seen of Van Morrison for a long time. He avoided public appearances, involving himself instead with studio experiments.

In 1977 and 1978, Morrison teamed up with Dr John, an American blues singer, to produce 'A Period of Transition' and 'Wavelength', the latter a pulsing rock album which reaffirmed Morrison as a major rock star. In the summer of 1979, his twelfth album, 'Into the Music', was released containing the hit single, 'Bright Side of the Road'.

'Beautiful Vision' (1982) was a well-produced rock album. Later works included 'Inarticulate Speech of the Heart' (1983), 'An Album Selection' (1984) garnered from sold-out concerts at Belfast's Grand Opera House, and 'A Sense of Wonder' (1985). In July 1984 he appeared on stage with Bob Dylan at a giant outdoor rock festival in Slane, Co. Meath.

Recorded over seven months in 1986 in California and London, 'No Guru, No Method, No Teacher' confirmed Morrison as a musician of huge stature. The album was one of his very best, with a powerful lyrical vision.

Recently, the moody image that 'Van the Man' presented to the world has softened. His Dublin concert at the Stadium (1989) showed a happier stage performer than history and legend suggest. Among the latest collaborators to work with Morrison was the poet, Paul Durcan. Their unique spoken and sung recollections of hours' listening to the radio is contained in the album, 'Enlightenment'. Morrison's latest work is a double album, 'Hymns to the Silence' (1991).

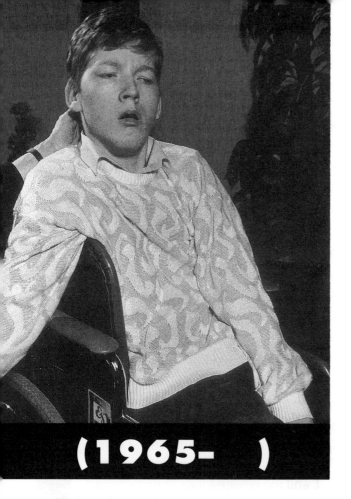

(1965-   )

Christopher Nolan was born in Mullingar, Co. Westmeath, on 6 September 1965. His father owned a farm, but was by profession a psychiatric nurse. Christopher's birth was an extremely difficult one, threatening the life of both mother and baby. As a result, the child was born with severe brain damage due to temporary lack of oxygen.

Although Christopher's body had useless limbs and uncoordinated movements, his mother, Bernadette, sensed that he had a sharp mind. The family began to communicate with him by eye contact. His mother arranged the alphabet letters all around the walls of her kitchen, illustrating each letter with one of her own drawings. Slowly, Christopher learned to spell by grouping these letters, indicating by eye movement which letter came next. His mother's fierce persistence was eventually rewarded when Christopher was examined by Dr Ciaran Barry, Medical Director of the Central Remedial Clinic in Dublin. When Dr Barry suggested that Christopher should attend the clinic, the Nolan family moved to Dublin. Doctors, teachers and occupational therapists worked tirelessly to develop his very limited powers of communication. He was also given special tests which showed he had above-average intelligence.

Christopher's life was transformed by a new drug which relaxed his tensed neck muscles and allowed partial control of his head movements for limited spells. The clinic designed a special 'Unicorn' stick which fitted to his forehead and let him type by jabbing the letters out with the end of the stick. His delighted family bought him an electric typewriter and his mother spent hours helping him to write, her hand steadying Christopher's chin. Christopher had now found a method by which he could express himself. He completed his first poem on 20 August 1977, 'I learn to bow', and within another day a second, 'I peer through ugliness'. Each word involved a ten-minute struggle, with a poem taking many days to complete. However, with practice, his work-rate increased. Christopher's mother was a constant inspiration and support. She steadied the uneven twitches of his head and shoulders, checked difficult words and spellings in the dictionary and understood the looks and nods that no one else could interpret.

Even in these early attempts, the range and accuracy of his expression, with frequent classical references, revealed verse throbbing with life, focused and powerful.

Christopher won the Spastics' Society Literacy Competition in 1979. Phil Odor, a computer scientist from Edinburgh, suggested that, by using a microcomputer, Christopher would be able to speed up his typing. When the *Sunday Times* launched an appeal for £2,200 to buy the machine, thousands of readers contributed more than £40,000. At Christopher's request, a trust was set up which allocated the surplus to buy computers for other disabled people. The machine proved to be an amazing success. It gave Christopher a great deal of freedom, allowed him to increase his work-rate, and enabled him to play computer games for relaxation.

Christopher wanted normal full-time education at an ordinary secondary school, and Mount Temple Comprehensive School enrolled him. The long school days were tiring, but Christopher received great support from teachers and caring friends. His first book, aptly titled *A Damburst of Dreams*, was released in 1981. His experiences at Mount Temple formed the basis of his autobiography, *Under the Eye of the Clock* (1987). The work is remarkable for its powerful imagery and total lack of self-pity. It won the Whitbread Book of the Year Award and the Whitbread Book Award. At eighteen, Christopher went to Trinity College, Dublin, leaving after a year to concentrate on his writing.

6 October 1989 saw the staging of his play, *Torchlight and Laser Beam* (co-written with Michael Scott), as part of that year's Dublin Theatre Festival. The play was based on Christopher's own poems and on *Under the Eye of the Clock*. He also formed the theatre company Heliotrope which later brought the play to Edinburgh, its first production outside Ireland. *Torchlight and Laser Beam* juxtaposes the values of the able-bodied against a secretly able-minded but physically handicapped person.

Even with the help of modern technology, Christopher's work-rate is painstakingly slow, each line taking hours of hard physical effort. His output so far is a remarkable testimony to an indomitable spirit and astonishing determination, as well as an extraordinary literary talent.

(1917-   )

Vincent O'Brien was born at Churchtown, Co. Cork, on 9 April 1917, the first child of his father's second family. His father Dan, a farmer, also kept horses for racing. Young Vincent soon developed an interest in the sport. Educated at Mungret College, Limerick, he later raced for a while as an amateur jockey with moderate success.

After his father's death in 1943, the farm was left to a son of Dan's first marriage. However, a rich businessman from England sent Vincent six horses for training at the farm which he rented from his half-brother.

O'Brien's first racing success was on the flat in Tipperary with a horse called Oversway. Within a year, his work resulted in a small financial reward for its owner. This modest success was O'Brien's springboard to a career of dazzling triumph as a trainer. His first big winner, Drybob, was at the Irish Cambridgeshire in 1944. Victories in the Cheltenham Gold Cup (four times), the Champion Hurdle (three times) and the Grand National (three times in succession) made O'Brien the most successful National Hunt trainer in Ireland and Britain within a few years.

In 1951, O'Brien moved to Ballydoyle, south of Cashel. He transformed the small, run-down estate into a superb, modern training centre with marvellous gallops and its own racecourse and grandstand. During the same year, he married an Australian, Jacqueline Witterton, a well-known racehorse photographer. They now have two sons and three daughters.

In 1953, Vincent O'Brien was Champion National Hunt trainer in England and also had the winner of the Irish Derby. Although banned in 1954, charged with holding back horses, and again in 1960 when his horse Chamour failed a drugs test, he vigorously protested his innocence on both occasions and came back when the sentences were lifted with a succession of victories at home and abroad.

During the late 1950s, O'Brien concentrated on flat racing, a change from the jumps which most trainers find difficult. Even so, he won the English St Leger (1957), the Arc de Triomphe and the King George VI and Queen Elizabeth Stakes (1958) with Ballymoss. Ballymoss, bought for 4,500 guineas, was sold at the end of his career for

250,000 guineas. This was just one of O'Brien's many shrewd investments.

O'Brien's success was relentless. He trained six Epsom Derby winners, a twentieth-century record, between 1962 and 1982. His horses also won many classic races in Ireland, England, France and America. These included the St Leger, the Prix de l'Arc de Triomphe, the 2000 Guineas, the 1000 Guineas, the Oaks, the Irish Sweeps Derby, the French Derby, King George VI and Queen Elizabeth Stakes, and the Irish Oaks. Some of the horses trained by O'Brien are now famous in racing history. They include Sir Ivor, Hatton's Grace, Cottage Rake, Early Mist, Royal Tan, Quare Times, Ballymoss, Larkspur, Roberto and Nijinsky.

The hallmarks of O'Brien's success include a unique versatility in handling horses for hurdles, fences and the flat. He also has an uncanny eye for potential in a horse and the ability to develop that potential. These talents are combined with a shrewd business sense, meticulous attention in training and, of course, luck.

Recently, O'Brien, Robert Sangster and John Magnier have built up Coolmore Stud, one of Europe's most prestigious stallion stations. In 1990, his horse Royal Academy won the Breeders Cup Mile. Now in his seventies, he is preparing to hand the reins over to his son, Charles, leaving him a daunting career to emulate.

VINCENT O'BRIEN

Vincent O'Brien (right) watches his 1954 Grand National winner 'Early Mist' on its return to Ireland after the race

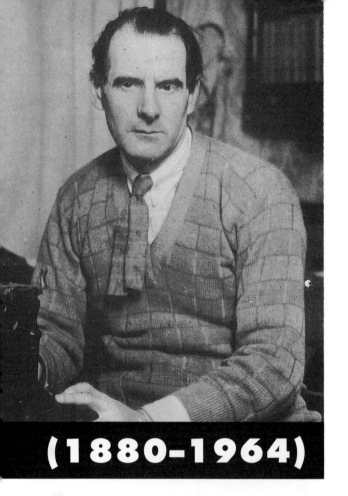

(1880-1964)

Sean O'Casey was born on 30 March 1880 at 85 Upper Dorset Street, Dublin. At the time, his native city had some of the worst slums in Europe. Disease raged like wildfire through the overcrowded tenements of the poor and the infant death rate was frightening. Three of O'Casey's brothers and sisters died in infancy. During his life he used several names. Born John Casey, he used the Irish version, Seán O'Cathasaigh, while involved with the Gaelic League; 'Casside' when speaking of himself in his autobiographies; and Sean O'Casey on his published plays.

O'Casey's childhood was tormented by eye ulcers which his mother soothed with ointment, drops and bandages. Although his sight improved somewhat, it remained weak

all his life. But no matter how sore his eyes might be, they were incredibly sharp. He observed the fine mansions and the slums, the joys and sorrows of street life, the images and impressions he would later describe so sharply in his plays. O'Casey's family lived near the slums but not in them. Even when his father died in 1886, starting the family's decline into genteel poverty, they still avoided the worst areas of Dublin.

Sean O'Casey's early life was a jigsaw of jobs and interests—clerk, stock boy, teacher and railway labourer. He joined the Gaelic League, the Irish Republican Brotherhood, the Irish Citizen Army, and learned Irish. He also acted, playing parts in melodramas in the Mechanics Theatre which was to become the Abbey.

Dismissed from the railway in 1911, O'Casey experienced the hardships of unemployment. He became active in trade unionism under the leadership of his hero, James Larkin, who demanded better conditions for workers.

O'Casey's first plays were rejected by the Abbey Theatre. Under Lady Gregory's encouragement, however, his play, *The Shadow of a Gunman*, was staged in 1923 with great success. In 1924 perhaps his greatest play, *Juno and the Paycock*, which dealt with the recent Civil War, played to packed houses at the Abbey. In 1926, *The Plough and the Stars* was performed amid protests over the way O'Casey showed the suffering caused by the 1916 Rising. None the less the play was sold out. He married the Irish actress, Eileen Carey, in 1927. They had three children.

O'Casey left for England in 1926. His next play, *The Silver Tassie*, which was rejected by the Abbey—a painful blow which he never forgave—opened in London in 1929 and later in New York, breaking box office records. None of his subsequent plays reached the heights of his first three major works.

O'Casey wrote six marvellous volumes of his life story, working right up to his death. Although nearly blind in his later years, he continued to write letters and articles, many speaking out against injustice and hypocrisy. O'Casey's plays, though set in poverty, show the triumph of man's spirit. He died in Torquay on 18 September 1964.

Sean O'Casey (right) in London with producer Sam Wanamaker

(1775-1847)

Daniel O'Connell was born on 6 August 1775 near Cahirciveen, Co. Kerry. He spent much of his early life with his uncle at Derrynane House near Waterville. An intelligent child, he was educated in Cobh, Co. Cork. Later he went to university in France because Catholics were not allowed into Trinity College at the time. He became a lawyer and was called to the Irish Bar in 1798. Having witnessed revolutionary violence in France, O'Connell believed that no cause was worth bloodshed. He himself was very upset when he had to kill a duelling opponent in 1815.

In 1800, Ireland lost its right to self-government under the Act of Union. In his first public speech, O'Connell opposed the Union. Repeal of the Act became one of his lifelong ambitions. His other mission, Catholic emancipation, aimed at ending the harsh penal laws which limited the voting rights and educational opportunities of the Catholic majority.

O'Connell set up many organisations to raise money for the cause of emancipation, including the Catholic Association which he founded in 1823. Supported by the clergy, the Association soon grew into a nationwide organisation. Funds poured in and O'Connell became very popular. When the British government tried to ban the Association, O'Connell simply changed its name. In 1828, O'Connell was elected to parliament in Co. Clare, defeating the government candidate. Because he was a Catholic, however, he was barred from taking his seat. The next year was a triumphant one for O'Connell, the 'Liberator', when Catholic emancipation was granted in April 1829.

Daniel O'Connell now embarked on repealing the Act of Union. In the opinion of the British government, this movement for Irish independence amounted to treason and Repeal was soundly defeated in a parliamentary vote. Meanwhile, O'Connell represented Dublin city in parliament and also became Dublin's first Catholic Lord Mayor.

O'Connell's Repeal Association included many men (Young Irelanders) who, unlike him, believed that independence could only be won by the use of force. In 1843, O'Connell held his first meeting to protest against the Act of Union in Trim, Co. Meath. Similar meetings drew such large crowds they were described as 'monster' rallies. Almost a million people listened to O'Connell's powerful voice on Tara Hill. Although he ensured that the huge crowds were orderly and peaceful, the government grew worried that trouble might break out. When O'Connell next planned a meeting on 8 October 1843 at Clontarf, near Dublin, the government placed soldiers around the field. Ever anxious to prevent bloodshed, O'Connell called off the protest rally. Trusting his judgment, the people obeyed him and a possible riot was avoided.

In 1844, O'Connell was arrested and charged with conspiracy. He was released after three months in jail. Weakened physically by overwork, disappointed by the failure of Repeal and worried over disagreements with the Young Irelanders, O'Connell sailed to France for health reasons. Before leaving, he appealed for help to deal with the terrible potato famine which was stalking the land.

The 'Liberator' died in Genoa, Italy, on 15 May 1847. At his own request, his heart was taken to Rome. His body was brought back to Ireland and buried under the round tower in Glasnevin Cemetery, Dublin.

Daniel O'Connell (centre, with black hair) takes his seat in the House of Commons

Grace O'Malley was born about 1530. She is also called Granuaile. A legend says this means 'Grainne of the cropped hair'. It tells how she cut off her hair as a child so her father, chieftain of the territory around Clew Bay in Mayo, would let her sail with him to Spain. The O'Malleys were a seafaring clan. In wooden galleys powered by sail or oar, they traded fish and cattle hides for iron, salt and wine. The young Grace lived in Belclare Castle near Westport or on Clare Island.

At sixteen Grace married a Galway chieftain, Donal O'Flaherty. They may have met just once before their wedding, which was arranged between the two families. Initially Grace seemed content to be mother of their three children, but she loved the sea

and even organised a fleet of ships, training the men herself. Her name became famous along the coastline. Soon it was Grace who was the real O'Flaherty chieftain.

Grace's husband, nicknamed Donal of the Battles, was constantly fighting with neighbouring clans. He defended a castle against the Joyces which was named Cock's Castle after him. When Donal died, the Joyces assumed they would take the castle. But Grace resisted so bravely that it was renamed Hen's Castle.

Grace was later besieged by English troops in her husband's castle at Benowen, Co. Galway. With her supplies dwindling, she ordered burning oil to be poured over the attackers. That night, she lit a fire and soon a chain of bonfires relayed her distress to Mayo, bringing her father's fleet to the rescue.

Grace returned to Clew Bay, a perfect hideout with a tricky current which was dangerous for strange vessels. By fishing, trading, charging passage fees and piracy, she became wealthy and soon led 200 men. She once landed at Howth near Dublin after a long voyage. Locking the gates, Lord Howth refused her food and shelter. Grace captured his son, releasing him on condition that the gates would remain open and that an extra place be set at table from then on. Grace's demands are honoured to this day.

Grace's second husband was Richard Bourke. They had one child, Tibbot na Long (Tibbot of the Ships), born aboard her ship. Shortly after the birth, Grace's galley was attacked by African pirates. Things looked bad until Grace charged on deck in her night clothes with a gun in one hand and a flaming torch in the other. The attackers were so shocked that Grace's men defeated them.

In 1584, Queen Elizabeth appointed Richard Bingham as Governor of Connacht. He wanted English rule established there where chieftains like Grace were resisting. For years he tormented her. In 1586 he imprisoned Grace and built a gallows to hang her. However, she was released in exchange for hostages. Bingham also confiscated 1,000 of her cattle.

Grace was getting older. Her ships were being watched, her movements followed. In dire straits, she gambled boldly. She wrote to Queen Elizabeth I complaining about Bingham. Elizabeth sent a list of questions which Grace carefully answered, not mentioning her piracy 'business'. In 1593 Grace undertook the long, risky voyage to London. Elizabeth eventually agreed to see her, and the two women, both battling for survival in a man's world, understood each other. Grace was allowed to continue her 'business' by land and sea.

Although Bingham continued to hound her, Grace lived to see her son, Tibbot, become a powerful lord. She died at the start of the new century, probably in the year 1603. The Gaelic world, weakened by the spreading power of English life and customs, died with her.

(1550-1616)

Hugh O'Neill was born at Dungannon, Co. Tyrone, in 1550. He lived in a world of Gaelic clan rivalry which was under constant threat of English domination. Hugh's father, Matthew O'Neill, was murdered to allow his half-brother, Shane, to become chieftain of the O'Neill clan. At the age of nine, Hugh was taken by the Queen's deputy, Sir Henry Sidney, and brought up as an English noble. Sidney was hopeful of Hugh's loyalty to the English crown when the young lad returned to Ulster in 1568. For a while Hugh seemed to take the English side. He led the Queen's cavalry against the Desmond Rebellion in 1569 and in 1573 assisted the Earl of Essex. By 1587 he was made Earl of Tyrone.

In 1588, however, Hugh disobeyed government instructions and gave assistance to survivors from wrecked Spanish ships, part of the mighty but doomed Armada which had come to invade England. Meanwhile, although allowed to keep only 600 soldiers, he soon built up a large army by steadily changing his troops.

In 1591, O'Neill married Mabel Bagenal, a daughter of Sir Henry Bagenal, a man who was at first a friend but who later became a bitter enemy. All this time, Hugh was training men, building up stores of weapons, and making agreements with neighbouring clans. In 1591, Hugh helped the escape of Red Hugh O'Donnell from Dublin Castle. By 1592, O'Neill had a huge army of 17,000 men at his command and before long was crowned The O'Neill.

Declared a traitor by the English government, O'Neill appealed for pardon, but was only playing for time until Spanish help arrived. However, this waiting game ended in 1595 when he destroyed an English fort in Armagh before defeating a government army at Clontibret, Co. Monaghan. O'Neill's advantage lay in the fact that he knew the countryside. The English were used to fighting with large armies on open ground. O'Neill, however, had trained his men in guerrilla warfare, launching surprise attacks before disappearing into marshy land or mountain. For a while there was an uneasy peace as both sides waited and strengthened their positions. But war broke out again in 1597 with O'Neill defeating the English at Benburb and later routing a large force in the Battle of the Yellow Ford near Armagh. Lord Bagenal was just one of the many who died at the Yellow Ford.

Worried about O'Neill's growing power, Queen Elizabeth sent the Earl of

Essex with 20,000 men to control Ulster. To her annoyance, Essex failed to defeat O'Neill. Summoned back to London, Essex was beheaded and Elizabeth replaced him with Lord Mountjoy, a ruthless soldier who was determined to crush O'Neill before Spanish aid arrived.

In September 1601, the long-expected Spanish Army of 3,000 men under Don Juan del Aguila landed at Kinsale, Co. Cork. Mountjoy immediately besieged Kinsale. O'Neill, O'Donnell and other northern chiefs arrived there in December after a long journey southwards. The English, sandwiched between the Spaniards and the Irish, were low in supplies. O'Neill wanted to wait until the English were weakened by exhaustion, hunger and wintry conditions, but O'Donnell and del Aguila wanted an immediate attack. The future of Gaelic Ireland was at stake. The Battle of Kinsale took place on Christmas Eve 1601. It ended in confusion, with the Irish and Spanish Armies routed. With his battered army, O'Neill struggled home. In March 1603, he surrendered to Mountjoy at Mellifont, Co. Louth.

With Ulster now under English administration and the Gaelic way of life disappearing, O'Neill decided to leave Ireland. In September 1607, with almost 100 other Gaelic chieftains, he sailed from Lough Swilly to exile in Europe, an event which is known as the Flight of the Earls. Hugh settled in Rome and was received with honour. He died there on 20 July 1616.

(1936-)

Tony O'Reilly was born in Griffith Avenue, Dublin, on 7 May 1936. He was educated at Belvedere College and later studied law in University College, Dublin. A brilliant student, he was an honours graduate in civil law and a qualified solicitor. He also earned a Ph.D. in agricultural marketing from the University of Bradford in England.

Tony O'Reilly was equally successful in sports. He received his first international rugby cap at the age of eighteen. In an impressive career, he played in the Irish colours twenty-nine times. Chosen to play for the Lions in ten international tests, he scored a record thirty-eight tries.

O'Reilly's rise to prominence in the world of business was meteoric leaving a dazzling trail of achievements. He was international consultant for Weston Evans (UK) from 1958 to 1960 and then worked for Suttons Ltd, Cork (1960–62), and McCowen's, Tralee (1961). He was then appointed General Manager of An Bord Bainne (the Dairy Board) (1962–66).

O'Reilly then rapidly progressed through the senior ranks of the Heinz company. From 1967 to 1970, he was joint managing director of Heinz Erin Ltd. By 1979 he held all the top offices in this massive food and nutrition company. Based in Pittsburgh in the USA, Heinz is one of the largest companies of its kind in the world. Under O'Reilly's shrewd guidance, it has grown by leaps and bounds.

He became Managing Director of the Sugar Company and of Erin Foods (1966–69).

O'Reilly's high-powered business schedule has set him at the helm of many other companies. These include Independent Newspapers and Fitzwilton plc. Fitwilton was recently involved in buying a substantial share of the interest in Waterford Wedgewood, the crystal and china company. He is also an investor in several Irish luxury hotels.

O'Reilly has served as director of several important organisations during his glittering career. These include Mobil Oil, Bankers Trust, Washington Post, Notre Dame University and Georgetown University. He has also been actively involved in several charitable and cultural organisations, especially the Irish Fund. He is Chairman and Founder of the American-Ireland Fund which contributes millions of pounds to finance many peace projects in Northern Ireland and which seeks to promote economic and cultural development throughout Ireland.

In 1963, he married Susan Cameron and has a family of six children. In September 1991, he married for a second time. His new wife is Christina Goulandris, a bloodstock breeder and member of a prominent Greek shipping family.

Ireland's premier international tycoon, Tony O'Reilly, is also a noted wit, story-teller and racehorse owner.

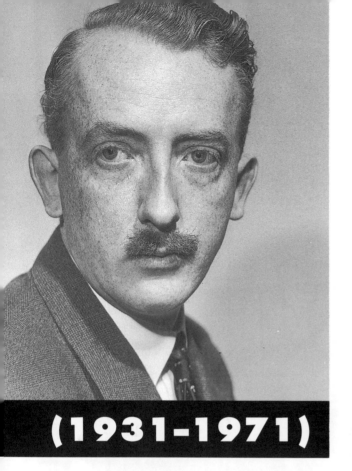

(1931-1971)

Seán Ó Riada (John Reidy) was born in Cork on 1 August 1931. He was the son of a Garda sergeant and was brought up in Bruff, Co. Limerick, where he learned the traditional fiddle. He was educated at the Christian Brothers School in Adare, and in St Munchin's College, Co. Limerick. He went to University College, Cork, from 1948 to 1952. While there, Ó Riada majored in classics and music, having earlier studied the piano and organ.

After receiving his B.Mus., Ó Riada continued his studies in France and Italy, and finally decided on a musical career. He was assistant director of music at Radio Éireann (1954–55), but resigned when he found that his work schedule was too routine and limiting. Instead, he decided to pursue the life of a freelance musician.

In 1955, Ó Riada returned to Ireland after spending time in France and Italy as a jazz pianist. He then became Musical Director of the Abbey Theatre and retained that position for the next seven years. This was a most productive period for Ó Riada. He arranged music for the Radio Éireann singers and Light Orchestra, and wrote original music for various orchestras. During this period, he adopted the Irish version of his name. This underlined his commitment to the Irish language and culture. Later, with his wife Ruth and their seven children, he moved to Cúil Aodha (Coolea), the Gaeltacht area west of Macroom, Co. Cork. Ó Riada was lecturer of music at University College, Cork, from 1963 to 1971.

Seán Ó Riada was responsible for the formation of Ceoltóirí Cualann, an Irish traditional music group, which was later to spawn the internationally famous Chieftains, as well as groups such as Horslips, Planxty and the Bothy Band. At a time when there was little interest in the Irish musical tradition, he revealed its riches by gathering together a group of master musicians and inspired them to play beyond the sum of their individual talents. In this way, Ó Riada altered the course of Ireland's musical culture. He brought new life to the music of west Cork and formed a local ensemble, the Cuil Aodha church choir, for which he wrote many sacred compositions, including a Requiem Mass.

By now he was a household name, having composed music for Gael Linn's well-received documentary film, *Mise Éire* (1959), which charted Ireland's fight for independence. Based on the tune, 'Róisín Dubh', Ó Riada's film music won first prize at the Cannes Film Festival. His Ceoltóirí Cualann received widespread acclaim at the opening of Dublin's Theatre Festival in 1962, further strengthening Ó Riada's reputation. In the following year, he composed the music for a film version of *The Playboy of the Western World*. He also gave a series of talks on Radio Éireann entitled, 'Our Musical Heritage', which analysed Irish music and its relationships with Eastern music. In 1968, he received the Composer of the Year award at the Belfast Committee.

Ó Riada's contribution to the development of Irish music is momentous. There is little question that he would have continued to expand his musical horizons had he not died at the age of forty years in a London hospital on 3 October 1971. His untimely death was a great loss to Irish music. His body was brought back to Cúil Aodha and buried in the churchyard of St Gobnait, Ballyvourney.

SEÁN Ó RIADA

(c.1130-1180)

Laurence O'Toole was born in Castledermot about 1130. Laurence's father, Murtagh, was a prince in Kildare. From an early age, the young boy was thrust into the ruthless world of twelfth-century Irish politics when Diarmuid MacMurrough, King of Leinster, forced Laurence's father to deliver up his son as a hostage. However, Murtagh managed to have his child transferred into the care of the Bishop of Glendalough. There, young Laurence decided to commit his life to the service of the Church. He spent many years in Glendalough and eventually took his final vows as a monk. At the age of twenty-five, Laurence was made Abbot of Glendalough. He declined the position of bishop, stating humbly that he was too young and inexperienced for the responsibility involved. In 1162, however, following the death of Bishop Gregory, Laurence was the popular choice to succeed him as Archbishop of Dublin.

The youthful Archbishop impressed everyone with his holiness and fairness. His wisdom was called upon when, in desperation, the people of Dublin asked him to negotiate with the Norman leader, Richard le Clare (Strongbow), during the siege of 1170. Laurence acted as mediator between Roderick O'Connor and Strongbow. However, to Laurence's horror, even as the discussions were taking place, the Norman soldiers had broken into the city, killing and burning. Archbishop O'Toole furiously denounced the treacherous attack. He urged the Irish chieftains to forget old quarrels and unite under O'Connor. In 1171, when King Henry II arrived in Ireland with a large army and papal support, Laurence acknowledged that Irish resistance was a futile sacrifice of life.

In 1175, Laurence O'Toole was responsible for the building of Christ Church Cathedral in Dublin. In 1179, he was asked to attend the Third Lateran Council by Pope Alexander III. O'Toole was appointed Papal Legate and given a document which gave papal protection to his Church in Ireland. He had only been allowed safe passage through Henry's kingdom after swearing that he would seek nothing at the Council that might adversely affect the King's interest.

Laurence O'Toole again found himself occupying the middle ground between O'Connor and Henry in 1180. However, relations between Laurence and the Norman king deteriorated when Henry, disliking the rights granted to the Church, blocked Laurence's return to Ireland. When the King travelled to France, Laurence followed in an effort to persuade him to lift the travel restrictions. But before he could obtain a meeting, Laurence died at Eu in France on 14 November 1180 and was declared a saint in 1226.

Christ Church Cathedral

(1846-1891)

Charles Stewart Parnell was born at Avondale, Co. Wicklow, on 27 June 1846. He was part of a wealthy Protestant family and enjoyed the comfortable lifestyle of a landlord. But all of this was soon to change.

Parnell's great-grandfather had opposed the 1800 Union with Britain. During his childhood, Parnell heard stories about the terrible famine of 1845–48 and the wasted sacrifice of the 1798 Rebellion. The execution of three Republicans known as the Manchester Martyrs (1867) convinced Parnell that Ireland needed political leadership.

In 1875, Parnell was elected to represent Co. Meath in the London parliament under the Irish Party leader, Isaac Butt. During Butt's leadership, the Irish representatives were only a tiny, powerless group in the House of Commons. They received little attention and even less support for their views. Parnell was determined to end this. He joined with Joseph Biggar from Cavan in interfering with parliamentary business, interrupting speeches and talking well beyond the permitted period for a topic. Using this strategy of 'obstruction', Parnell and Biggar focused attention on Irish affairs. After Butt's death, Parnell led the Irish Party. He was a poor speaker, but trained himself to address the huge crowds that flocked to hear their 'Chief'.

Meanwhile the ideas of the Land League, established by Michael Davitt in 1879 to obtain improved conditions for tenant farmers, had spread across the country. Although a Protestant landlord himself, Parnell firmly supported the League's efforts.

Trouble over rent payments soon broke out in certain areas of the country. Because of his activities with the League, Parnell was imprisoned without trial in Kilmainham Jail. But when the League's activities grew stronger, he and other arrested Land League leaders were released in 1882. Parnell promised to support the English Liberal Party if they passed laws to improve conditions for Irish tenant farmers.

There were many differences among those who were fighting for Irish freedom. The Fenians used violence as a means to obtain independence. Parnell, the landlord, was fighting for fair treatment of tenants. And Davitt believed that Irish land belonged to Irish people. Parnell's main political ambition was Home Rule—an Irish parliament in

Dublin. In the 1885 elections, Parnell's party won eighty-five seats. The Liberal Party took office under William Gladstone only because Parnell's eighty-five members joined them to outnumber the Conservatives. Parnell's price for this support was that Gladstone would introduce a Home Rule Bill. Although Gladstone himself felt that this was a reasonable demand, not all of his party agreed. In 1886, Gladstone's Home Rule Bill was defeated and the Liberals fell from power.

In 1887, *The Times* newspaper in London accused Parnell of supporting the assassination of the Chief Secretary of Ireland in the Phoenix Park. The evidence against him turned out to be a letter to the paper which had been forged by Richard Pigott. Parnell's popularity soared when people learned the truth about the 'Pigott Forgeries'.

In 1890, Captain William O'Shea, a former member of Parnell's party, obtained a divorce from his wife Katharine. Parnell had been living with Katharine for years, and Captain O'Shea had finally decided to make the case public. Many of Parnell's own party deserted him when they heard about this. The Liberals ended their parliamentary partnership with the Irish Party. In December 1890, Parnell's own party voted against him remaining on as their leader.

Trying to rally support, Parnell travelled the country. But the 'Uncrowned King', weakened by worry and exhaustion, died at the age of forty-five at Brighton on 6 October 1891. He had married

Katharine just five months earlier. In ten years of power and national popularity, Parnell had given the country self-respect and had developed the political desire for national independence and land reform.

CHARLES STEWART PARNELL

(c.390-461)

The life of St Patrick, Ireland's patron saint, is clouded and uncertain. Early manuscripts disagree on even the date of his birth and death. Much of what we know about him comes from his book, *Confessions*, his letter to Coroticus protesting against slave-traders, and a prayer in Irish called the *Breastplate of St Patrick*.

Patrick was born towards the end of the fourth century, possibly near the mouth of the River Severn in Roman Britain. He was the son of a Roman official. At sixteen, he was captured by Irish raiders and sold to a chieftain called Milchiu in Antrim. There he herded pigs and sheep at a place usually identified with Slemish Mountain in Co. Meath. Speaking Latin, Patrick had to learn the Celtic language. He sought comfort from loneliness and hardship in regular prayer.

After six years of slavery, Patrick escaped. Making the long dangerous journey to Wexford, he boarded a merchant ship which had appeared to him beforehand in a dream. He converted the crew when he saved them from starvation. It was the beginning of a lifetime's missionary work.

Patrick's parents were overjoyed to see their long-lost son again. They pressed him to stay, but Patrick had other plans. In a dream, he heard the Irish people calling on him to return and convert them to Christianity. Patrick decided to enter the priesthood and was ordained by St Amator.

In 431, Palladius had been appointed first bishop of Ireland, but he died inside a year. Patrick was then sent to convert the Celts who worshipped many gods, including the sun. Patrick is thought to have landed at the mouth of the River Boyne where he baptised the local ruler, Dichiu. Dichiu presented Patrick with land and a barn which became Patrick's first church.

Patrick chose Armagh as his headquarters—to this day, Armagh remains the ecclesiastical capital of Ireland. His mission was difficult. Local chieftains were suspicious and the Celtic druids distrusted the new religion. More than once Patrick was imprisoned, sometimes escaping by giving gifts or winning his captor's friendship.

Patrick was fearless and unconcerned about his personal comfort or safety. His knowledge of the Celtic language helped him spread the Christian message wherever he went. He baptised converts, ordained priests and organised Christian communities. Churches had to be built, copies of the Bible handwritten, page by page, vestments needed to be made, holy bread baked and altar wine shipped from the Continent.

Patrick's life was shrouded in legends. Whether or not he banished snakes from Ireland, used a three-leaved shamrock to explain the Holy Trinity or lit a paschal fire at Slane to defy the pagan light on Tara, it is certain that Patrick spread Christianity throughout the country. Countless holy wells, churches, abbeys and places of pilgrimage are named after him. His bell and its shrine, as well as an enshrined tooth, are on display in the National Museum in Dublin. His enshrined arm can be seen in St Patrick's Church, Belfast.

The date of Patrick's death is also uncertain. Some annals say 493, but most sources agree on the year 461. Patrick is believed to have been buried in Downpatrick. His feast day on 17 March is celebrated in many countries throughout the world. The principal cathedral of New York city is dedicated to St Patrick.

(1879–1916)

join the Gaelic League in 1895. Although he was called to the bar after his graduation from the Royal University in 1901, he seldom practised. His time was occupied in helping his younger brother, William, run the family business and teaching Irish at University College, Dublin. From 1903 to 1908, Pearse was editor of the Gaelic League journal, *An Claidheamh Soluis*. Later, to improve his Irish, he built a cottage at Rosmuc in the Connemara Gaeltacht, where he spent his summer holidays.

Having a keen interest in education, in 1908 Pearse opened a bilingual school for boys in the Dublin suburb of Rathmines called Scoil Éanna (St Enda's, after the patron saint of the Aran Islands). The project was such a success that Pearse had to move his school to a larger building in Rathfarnham in 1910.

Over the next few years, Pearse travelled throughout Europe reviewing different methods of education. His attention was particularly focused on the Belgian system where bilingualism was in operation. His ambition for Scoil Éanna was to provide a model of education which would develop the child's mind, letting it grow creatively towards its own potential rather than forcing it into uniformity. It is only in recent years that this child-centred approach has been put into general practice in Irish primary education.

At Scoil Éanna, Pearse also advanced his ideal of a free and Gaelic Ireland. In 1913, with Eoin MacNeill and others, he formed the Irish Volunteers and joined the secret Irish Republican Brotherhood (IRB).

Patrick Henry Pearse was born on 10 November 1879 at 27 Great Brunswick Street (now renamed Pearse Street). Pearse's mother came from Co. Meath. His father, an English stonemason who settled in Dublin, had been attracted there by the employment prospects offered by a spate of church-building following Catholic emancipation.

Pearse received his early education at a local private school and then enrolled at Westland Row Christian Brothers School. It was during his schooldays that Pearse's love of the Irish language began. This led him to

Before long, he was made a member of its supreme council. In 1915 Pearse delivered a famous speech at the grave of the old Fenian, O'Donovan Rossa. His address ended: 'The fools, the fools, the fools! They have left us our Fenian dead, and while Ireland holds these graves, Ireland unfree shall never be at peace.'

Pearse helped to plan the 1916 Rising. He felt that a blood sacrifice was needed to secure Irish freedom, even though many others wished to wait until there were better opportunities for a military victory. It was Pearse who read the Proclamation of the Irish Republic outside the General Post Office in Dublin on Monday 24 April 1916. This signalled the beginning of the Easter Rising. During the Rebellion, Pearse was Commander-in-Chief of the Irish forces and President of the provisional government. Following a week of intense street fighting which caused much death and destruction, he called on his men to surrender unconditionally to the numerically superior British Army.

Following a court martial for his part in the Easter Rising, Pearse was executed by firing squad in Kilmainham Jail on 3 May 1916. Fourteen other prominent members of the Rising were also executed including his brother, Willie.

During his short life, Pearse translated much Irish poetry and wrote plays, poetry and stories. His play, *The Singer*, was staged at the Abbey in 1942. His Irish writings were collected in *Scríbhinní* (1919). Pearse's theories on education are described in *The Story of a Success* (1917), which recorded the history and development of Scoil Éanna.

In order to prevent the further slaughter of Dublin citizens, and in the hope of saving the lives of our followers now surrounded and hopelessly outnumbered, the members of the Provisional Government present at Head-Quarters have agreed to an unconditional surrender, and the Commandants of the various districts in the City and Country will order their commands to lay down arms.

P. H. Pearse
29th April 1916
3.45 p.m.

(1854-1932)

Horace Plunkett was born in Gloucestershire, England, on 24 October 1854. He was the third son of Baron Dunsany. Plunkett was educated at Eton and later in Oxford, where he captained the university chess team and was a keen golfer. As a young man, he was afflicted with weak lungs, a form of tuberculosis. At the age of 25, seeking an outdoor, healthy lifestyle, he became a rancher in America, working in the foothills of the Rocky Mountains. He returned home to Dunsany, Co. Meath, each winter during his ten years in America and finally came home to stay in 1889. His experience with American agriculture had broadened his horizons and made him determined to reform agriculture in Ireland.

Plunkett championed the cause of agricultural co-operation among dairy farmers, especially in Munster. He established the first co-operative creamery in Drumcolliher, Co. Limerick. Plunkett dedicated himself to raising economic standards in farming and to improving the quality of Irish rural life. In 1891, he was appointed to the new Congested Districts Board. Although he considered himself a social reformer rather than a politican, Plunkett was elected as a Unionist MP candidate for South Co. Dublin in 1892. In 1894, he was made the first President of the Irish Agricultural Organisation Society. *The Irish Homestead* was launched by Plunkett in 1895 to provide news of the co-operative movement.

Plunkett's energetic planning and canvassing finally bore fruit in 1899 with the establishment of the Department of Agriculture and Technical Instruction for Ireland. As Vice-president, he steered the department in its vital early years. He hoped to introduce scientific methods to Irish agriculture, reorganise rural business along co-operative lines and restore self-reliant optimism to farmers. These three aims were neatly summed up in his famous slogan—'Better Farming, Better Business, Better Living'. With a mixture of idealism and shrewd business sense, he established a co-operative movement supported by Protestants and Catholics, by Nationalists and Unionists alike.

Plunkett was re-elected President of the Irish Agricultural Organisation Society in

1907. As a token of appreciation for his service to agriculture, he was given a house at 84 Merrion Square—Plunkett House—which was to become the headquarters of the Agricultural Co-operative Organisation. During the period 1908 to 1913, co-operatives around the country grew to almost a thousand with an annual turnover of over £3 million.

A firm supporter of Home Rule, Plunkett believed that a united Ireland would survive best within the British Commonwealth. He set up the Irish Dominion League as a means of achieving this political end. Becoming a member of the new Irish senate in 1922, he travelled widely, lecturing on agricultural co-operation. During a visit to the United States, his home at Foxrock, Co. Dublin, was burned by anti-Treaty forces in the Civil War. Plunkett then moved to England. In 1924 he chaired a conference on co-operative farming in Wembley. In the following year he travelled to South Africa to promote the movement there.

Plunkett wrote many pamplets on agriculture. His two major works were *Ireland in the New Century* (1904) and *The Rural Life Problem of the United States* (1910). Two main interests dominated his life: the improvement of Irish agriculture and the maintenance of a united Ireland within the British Commonwealth. Although his last decade was shadowed by exile from Ireland, he never abandoned his constructive vision of his country's future. Sir Horace Plunkett died in Weybridge in Surrey on 26 March 1932.

Kilmeaden Creamery, Co. Waterford in the 1930s

SIR HORACE PLUNKETT

(1925-)

Maureen Potter was born on 3 January 1925 in Fairview, Dublin. She was the youngest of three children. Her father, a traveller for Mobil Oil, died when Maureen was just seven. Her mother won medals for singing. When she was five, Maureen entered the local St Mary's National School and from her first day there, began Irish dancing classes. At home, there were frequent musical evenings with neighbours and relatives around the family piano.

Maureen made her stage début in the Queen's Theatre, performing a song and dance act in a variety show. Her first professional pantomime, *Jack and the Beanstalk*, was staged in the Olympia in 1935. From there, while still at school, she left to work in the Theatre Royal which had just opened. In 1936, following an audition with the Jack Hylton Band, the twelve-year old, using an older friend's birth certificate, toured England and Germany. She returned to the London Palladium in September 1939.

On her return to Ireland, Maureen's breakthrough came when she was given the role of Man Friday in *Robinson Crusoe*. She starred with another great comedian, Jimmy O'Dea, who was to have a great influence on Maureen. When Jimmy's partner left, Maureen stepped in and gradually began to develop a comedy act with him. This famous partnership lasted until O'Dea's death in 1954.

During World War II, while Jimmy was away entertaining the troops, Maureen worked in Dublin's baroque theatre, the Capital, in a variety show. There she met Jack O'Leary who was to become her husband.

Although concentrating on the world of pantomime and variety, Maureen did not neglect straight acting. She worked with Mícheál Mac Liammóir and Hilton Edwards in several plays. But to generations of Irish children (and adults), the name of Maureen Potter is synonymous with winter pantomime. Her uproariously funny portrayals of Dublin characters and her satirical jokes about politicians in a string of Gaiety pantomimes (over forty-four seasons) have made her a household name. She also starred in her own summer show, 'Gaels of Laughter', for an unbroken run of eighteen seasons.

One of Maureen's busiest Christmases was when playing Man Friday to Jimmy O'Dea's Robinson Crusoe. When another actress, the Fairy Queen, became ill, Maureen had to play both parts, making very quick costume and make-up changes several times during the show. She was the comedienne chosen for the opening night of RTE 2. Her films include: *The Rising of the Moon, Gideon's Day* and two Joycean films, *Ulysses* and *Portrait of the Artist*. She has received many tributes including the Freedom of the City of Dublin in 1984. In March 1988, she received an honorary doctorate from Trinity College, Dublin, in recognition of her lifelong service to Irish entertainment. Recently she has returned to straight acting with phenomenal success, playing in Sean O'Casey's *Juno and the Paycock*, in Richard Brinsley Sheridan's *The School for Scandal*, as well as in two plays by Samuel Beckett, *Foot falls* and *Rockaby*, which were part of the 1991 Beckett Festival. In 1992, she starred in Hugh Leonard's play *Moving* at the Abbey Theatre.

A total professional, Maureen Potter now continues work despite recurrent arthritis which has entailed hip and knee operations. She has worked as associate director to a recent production of the pantomine, *Cinderella*, in her beloved Gaiety and has written a popular children's book, *The Theatre Cat* (1986). She lives in Clontarf with her husband and two sons. A much-loved Dubliner, she has captured the hearts of Irish audiences for over half a century.

Maureen as Mother Ireland

MAUREEN POTTER

(1762-1844)

Edmund Ignatius Rice was born on 1 June 1762 at Westcourt, near Callan, Co. Kilkenny. At the time, the harsh Penal Laws which had been enforced against Catholics for almost seventy years were slowly beginning to ease. Despite this, there were still no proper primary schools for Catholics. As a result, Edmund received his early education at a local hedge school from an Augustinian friar. In 1777, he went to a boarding school in Kilkenny where he remained for two years. At the age of seventeen, he was sent to Waterford as an apprentice to his uncle, a prosperous meat exporter and ship's chandler. Waterford at this time was a bustling shipping port. After his uncle's death, Edmund took over the business, running it very successfully for many years. He married in 1785, but his wife died shortly after the birth of their daughter four years later.

Throughout these years, Rice's mind had not been totally occupied with business. He took time to visit the sick, the imprisoned and poor people of the town. There were little or no educational opportunities for the poorer section of the Catholic population. He decided that something had to be done to ease their plight. So in 1796, with a group of friends, he set up a society to help adults who were in need of food and money. He had considered joining an Augustinian monastery in Rome, but realised that his mission was to be in Ireland. Encouraged by the local bishops and by Pope Pius VI, he began teaching poor young boys, using a business premises in Waterford. In 1802, he rented a stable and converted it into a schoolroom. Because the demand for learning was huge, Rice and his two assistant teachers were kept very busy indeed. In 1803 he abandoned his business career and concentrated instead on teaching. When the stable room proved unsatisfactory as a place of learning, he built a new schoolroom at Mount Sion, Waterford, in 1804, helped by friends and by the local bishop. There were financial worries initially, but by 1805 two new schools in Clonmel and Dungarvan had been established. In 1808, Rice and his colleagues took religious vows and followed rules similar to the code of the Presentation nuns. Each one took a new name and Edmund became Edmund Ignatius Rice. His Order was to transform the face of Irish education.

In 1809, the new Order set up its first school in Cork. Soon his schools spread to Dublin. In 1820, Pope Pius VII gave his approval to the order which was called the Institute of the Brothers of the Christian Schools of Ireland. Brother Ignatius was unanimously elected as Superior General in 1822, a position he held until his retirement in 1838.

Rice was very friendly with Charles Bianconi, who had arrived in Waterford with little money, and with the 'Liberator', Daniel O'Connell. O'Connell performed the opening ceremony of the Christian Brothers School, North Richmond Street, Dublin, in front of 100,000 people.

In 1828, Rice moved his headquarters to Dublin. His Christian Brothers schools were opening all over the country and also, since 1825, in England. In 1835, a Christian Brothers School was established in Gibraltar. In 1837, a British Royal Commission which was examining the state of Irish education praised the work being done by the Christian Brothers. When Rice retired in 1838, the Brothers had twenty-two houses in Ireland and England.

Edmund Ignatius Rice spent the last years of his energetic life in Mount Sion, where, after his death on 29 August 1844, he was buried. Since his death many more schools have been established in Ireland, England, Australia, America and South Africa.

O'Connell's Schools, Dublin

(1944-   )

Mary Robinson was born on 21 May 1944 in Ballina, Co. Mayo. She is the daughter of Dr Aubrey Bourke, GP and Dr Tessa Bourke (née O'Donnell).

Mary received her first education in a small local school. At the age of ten, she went as a boarder to Mount Anville in Dublin. After a year in Paris, she entered Trinity College, Dublin. From there she went to King's Inns and was granted an LL.M. First Class at Harvard University in America. Called to the Irish Bar in 1967, she became a Master of Law the following year.

In 1969, Mary was appointed Reid Professor of Law at Trinity College, Dublin. She was the youngest person ever to hold that office. That same year, against great odds, she secured a Seanad seat on the Dublin University panel and retained it for the next two decades, having joined the Labour Party.

Mary Robinson's legislative and political contribution to the Senate is a most impressive one. She served for many years on the Joint Committee on EC Legislation and is recognised as a leading expert on European Law. She played a prominent part on the New Ireland Forum, served on the Oireachtas Committee on marital breakdown, and was the first President of the Women's Political Association and a former President of Cherish—the representative body for single parents. In 1989, she was elected Mayo Person of the Year and represented Ireland in the Women of Europe Award the previous year.

Her legal achievements have been equally impressive. She was a member of the International Commission of Jurists, a body composed of renowned human rights lawyers. She was also on the board of the Common Market Law Review and the European Air Law Association, further testimony to her expertise.

Mary Robinson has played a central role in several major constitutional and human rights case in both Irish and European courts. These include: the Reynolds Case which fought for the right of 18-year olds to vote; the de Burca Case which challenged the existing jury system for discrimination against women; the Wood Quay Case establishing the Dublin site as a national monument and ensuring archaeological exploration before building work proceeded;

the Murphy Case which was responsible for changing the way married couples were taxed; the Kennedy and Arnold Case which investigated the illegal tapping of journalists' telephones; the Derrynaflan Chalice Case which established the state's right to treasure trove; the Hyland Case ensuring equality of social welfare benefits for married couples; the Airey Case in which Ireland was found to be in breach of the Convention of Human Rights for failing to provide civil legal aid; and the Johnston Case which was central in changing the treatment of children born outside marriage. She was responsible for major changes in civil rights, representing travellers, unmarried mothers, homosexuals and students, whose rights were all championed by her.

In 1990, nominated by the Labour Party and supported by the Workers' Party and the Greens, Mary Robinson was declared a presidential candidate. Refusing to be labelled as a socialist, she was widely supported, not alone by women but by all shades of political opinion in Ireland. Building up a small but impressive election team, she swept to victory on 7 November 1990 with 52.8 per cent of the nationwide vote, winning 25 of the 41 constituencies. Her election as Ireland's first woman president attracted wide national and international interest. It represented a landmark in the life of modern Ireland, motivating women and young people. Mary Robinson is married to Nicholas Robinson, a solicitor, and they have three children.

MARY ROBINSON

(1959-   )

Stephen Roche was born on 28 November 1959 in Dundrum, Dublin. At fifteen, he became an apprentice fitter before working for Premier Dairies. By this time he was cycling regularly with the Dublin club, Orwell Wheelers, under his coach, Noel O'Neill, and establishing himself on the amateur circuit. Having won the Ras Tailteann in 1979, he decided to go to France and ride with a full-time amateur team in preparation for the 1980 Moscow Olympics where he finished 45th in the road race.

When Stephen won the Paris–Roubaix and the Paris–Reims classics, he was offered a contract by Peugeot. He decided to take on the challenge of professional cycling in 1981. He began as a domestique,

a cyclist who gives support to the star riders in the team. Roche was under the shadow of his fellow Irishman and rival, Sean Kelly, who had been scorching a trail of successes since 1977. Soon, however, Roche was making his own mark, winning the Paris to Nice in his first year.

In 1983, Stephen Roche received the white jersey as best newcomer in his first Tour de France. In 1985, he finished in third place, attracting some of the attention hitherto directed exclusively at Kelly. However, the following year was a disappointment. Troubled by a knee injury, he came 48th in the Tour de France. Following surgery, he redoubled his efforts and won the Tour de Valencia and the 2,000-mile Tour of Italy. Only four other cyclists in the history of the sport had won the Tour of Italy and the Tour de France in the same season. Roche was determined to join that elite group. The gruelling course presented a huge challenge to the competitor, taking him to the ultimate, physically and mentally. As the stages wore on, the race developed into a duel between Roche and Pedro Delgado. After twenty days of demanding effort, Delgado took the lead, but the Dubliner produced a superhuman performance at the end of the La Plagne stage, an effort which left him totally exhausted, needing oxygen to recover. However, his fierce will to win saw him back in the saddle the next day. Holding off Delgado's challenge in the final time-trial at Dijon, he rode into Paris in the yellow jersey, speeding up the Champs Elysées to victory. Roche was the first Irishman to win this famous cycling race.

From this triumph, it was on to Villach, Austria, for the World Championship. Roche was understandably drained after his hectic season, so his initial strategy was to help Sean Kelly take the title that had eluded him over his long career. By the closing stages, with Kelly fading, Roche decided that he himself could win. He did so with a final surge which left Kelly in fifth place.

In an astonishing season during which he cycled 27,000 miles, Roche had won the grand slam (Tour of Italy, Tour de France and the World Championship). He was the first cyclist to achieve the treble since the legendary Eddy Merckx in 1974. Stephen was later made a Freeman of Dublin, the first sportsman to be so honoured. Since that heady period, Roche's form has suffered because of a recurring knee injury, leaving him struggling to get back to top form. In March 1991, Roche won the Catalan race in Spain. He has established his own management company and co-wrote his autobiography, *Stephen Roche, the Agony and the Ecstasy*. In November 1991, he signed a new two-year contract with the Italian team, Carrera.

(1936-   )

Tony Ryan was born on 2 February 1936. He was the eldest son of a Thurles train driver. Transport featured prominently in the Ryan family history—his great-grandfather had been a coach builder for Bianconi, who introduced the country's first public transport system, and his grandfather was a station master.

Educated at the Christian Brothers School in Thurles, Ryan joined Aer Lingus in 1955 as a dispatcher at Shannon Airport. The nineteen-year old established himself quickly and before long was promoted. He spent periods in London and Chicago where he undertook night courses in business administration. Returning to Dublin in 1972, he became leasing manager for Aer Lingus. His breakthrough came the following year when Aer Lingus was trying to recover losses arising out of a slump in tourism due to the Northern Ireland troubles. The airline decided to rent a surplus Boeing 747 jumbo jet. Through persistence, drive and persuasion, Ryan managed to persuade Air Siam, who were looking for a Boeing 707, to lease the larger plane by accommodating it into a new route he himself proposed. The initial deal was impressive enough. But when the new Air Siam route quickly began to make a profit, Ryan's reputation within the international aviation industry soared.

Ryan was encouraged by his success. In 1975 he secured an agreement with Aer Lingus, in partnership with the London bank group, Guinness Peat, to finance his plans for a new aircraft company, Guinness Peat Aviation (GPA). His own initial share investment (£5,000) is now worth £20 million, reflecting GPA's phenomenal growth.

Many airlines around the world, seeking to avoid the heavy expenditure involved in buying an aircraft, welcomed the facility for short-term leasing offered by Ryan's company. GPA also financed the machines, leaving the airlines free to concentrate on strengthening their cargo and passenger routes.

Soon the Shannon-based company had amassed its own aircraft fleet which it leased to its customers. It had moved into the profitable North American market, where struggling airlines were desperate to cut back on their losses. They rushed to sell their aircraft and leased replacement planes instead.

In April 1986, Ryan's business expertise raised $340 million in London, New York and Tokyo to expand his fleet to almost three hundred aircraft by 1991, making it one of the world's largest aviation companies. Ryan's leasing arrangements have saved several airlines from ruin. They have contributed handsomely to the success of many more, and have resulted in huge profits for his own company, with assets of more than $2 billion.

Also in 1986 he established the Ryanair airline which, despite financial problems, brought competitive airfares on the Irish Sea route.

Ryan is ruthless in his determination and has amazing vitality. He spends much time travelling, recharging his energy at his farm in Dolla, north Tipperary, where he breeds pedigree cattle. He has also amassed an impressive collection of Irish art. In 1986, Limerick NIHE bestowed an honorary doctorate on Ryan in recognition of his achievements. His interest in the arts has resulted in his granting many significant awards and busaries. GPA has financed such events as the Chinese Warriors exhibition, the GPA Emerging Artists Awards and the ROSC exhibition. The company has also invested in the work of promising as well as estab--lished Irish artists.

TONY RYAN

(c.1655-1693)

Patrick Sarsfield was probably born at Lucan around 1655. His mother was descended from a long line of militant Irish chieftains. It was not surprising, therefore, that Sarsfield chose a military career.

He received his early military education in a French academy, getting his commission around 1672. On the death of his elder brother, William, in 1675, Patrick came into a legacy worth £2,000 yearly. In 1678 he was promoted to captain in Sir Thomas Dongan's Regiment of the Foot. He served under Marshal Luxembourg before returning to England where he received a commission in Charles II's Regiment of Guards. In 1681, the young officer sprang to public notice when he challenged Lord Grey to a duel, although the challenge was not accepted.

With James II on the throne of England in 1685, Sarsfield was again called into active service under the Duke of Marlborough at the Battle of Sedgemoor in defence of King James.

He was badly wounded and his men were routed. For the next two years Sarsfield served in the Horse Guards and also spent time in Ireland helping Ulster chieftains raise an army for King James. He became a Colonel of the Irish Dragoons and was eventually sent to England with his forces to counter an invasion by William of Orange. After a brief unsuccessful skirmish, James fled to France leaving William to be crowned King.

James's only hope of regaining his crown lay in Ireland and France. Still unswerving in his loyalty, Sarsfield followed his monarch to France where he remained until 1689. In that year a French fleet bearing James and Sarsfield arrived in Kinsale in March and proceeded to Dublin. The Ulster Protestants retreated to Derry and managed to hold out despite a 105-day siege. When Williamite reinforcements under Schomberg arrived, the Jacobites (James's army) retreated from Ulster. On 1 June Sarsfield, leading a small band of 500, was defeated by a strong force of Protestants. A further defeat followed at Ballyshannon. He was sent into Connacht where he succeeded in raising 2,000 men, and defeated Schomberg's army, thus securing Connacht for James. With his success, recruits poured into the Jacobite camp. However, they were only half-armed, half-trained and poorly led.

On 14 June 1690 William arrived at Carrickfergus with a well-equipped army of 35,000 experienced troops and reached the Boyne on 30 June. The Battle of the Boyne took place on 1 July and ended with defeat for James, who again fled to France.

The Jacobites regrouped in Limerick. Sarsfield's raid and destruction of William's siege train of cannon and explosives at Ballyneety is probably the best remembered episode of the entire war. With 600 cavalry, he rode out of Limerick to Killaloe where he crossed the river. On the night of 11 August, guided by the Rapparee, Galloping Hogan, they surprised the escort party of 100. Powder and guns were quickly exploded. William brought more cannon and the siege of Limerick began. However, the Jacobites managed to hold out to the end. Sarsfield was responsible for the defence of Galway, Sligo and Athlone. When the Williamite Commander, Ginkel, attempted to cross the River Shannon at Lanesborough he was defeated after Sarsfield had alerted the Irish garrison. He was rewarded for his loyalty when James created him Earl of Lucan and Commander-in-Chief in February 1691.

In May 1691 General St Ruth, an experienced French leader, arrived in Limerick. Learning that Ginkel's next target was Athlone, the new commander moved his army of 22,000 men there. He and Sarsfield quarrelled over the battle

plan and due to St Ruth's mishandling of the situation, Athlone was taken by Ginkel. After a further defeat at Aughrim, Limerick was besieged for the second time within a year. Eventually on 3 October 1691 a treaty was signed which brought the war to an end. Along with other Irish leaders (the Wild Geese) Sarsfield left for France.

His military career continued, fighting against his old enemy at the Battle of Steenkirke under Luxembourg. Luxembourg raised him to the rank of marshal in April 1693. Field Marshal Patrick Sarsfield was killed on 23 July 1693 at Landen, Belgium.

(1874-1922)

Ernest Shackleton was born at Kilkea, Co. Kildare on 15 February 1874, the son of a farmer. In 1880 his father left farming to study medicine at Trinity College, Dublin. Later the family moved to London where Ernest was educated at Dulwich College.

He studied to become a master mariner and passed his examination for first mate in 1896. Hearing that Captain Robert Scott was organising an expedition to the Antarctic he decided to join and sailed from England aboard the *Discovery* in 1901. Shackleton's job was to conduct scientific experiments on sea salt at different locations. In February 1902, when *Discovery* was locked in by ice, Scott decided to use the stranded ship as a base, and with two companions, reached 82° 16', further south than anyone had ever been before, after a difficult dangerous journey.

His adventure with Scott made Shackleton ambitious, and in 1907 he led his own expedition in the *Nimrod*, a whaler, to the Antarctic. There were fifteen members on board. On 29 October 1908 (spring in the southern hemisphere), Shackleton and three of the party set off with ponies and sledges for the South Pole. It was a horrific trek through blizzards with temperatures of minus thirty. Soon supplies began to run out, but Shackleton kept on course until they came within 100 miles of the Pole.

When he returned to England he was welcomed as a hero. He wrote a book about his experiences and lectured around the country. He was knighted and given £20,000 to organise another expedition. However, his dream of being the first to reach the South Pole was frustrated when this was achieved by the Norwegian, Amundsen, in 1912, and then by Captain Scott who died on the way back.

Shackleton then decided to cross the Antarctic continent from one side to the other. His ship, the *Endurance*, headed south in 1914 carrying new equipment including propeller-driven sledges. By January 1915 the ship was trapped in the ice which was pressing in on every side. As the Antarctic winter wore on, the pressure grew greater, until finally the *Endurance* broke up and sank.

Stranded thousands of miles from rescue, Shackleton led his men for five months across the ice packs until they reached Elephant Island which was totally uninhabited. Shackleton then picked five men and set off in a 20-foot boat to sail the 800-mile journey across the roughest, coldest seas in the world, to South Georgia, the nearest inhabited island.

The daunting journey proved Shackleton to be one of the bravest commanders in maritime history. Even when he reached South Georgia he had to cross mountains and glaciers 10,000 feet high to get help.

By May 1917 Shackleton was back in London. During World War I he was given the job of transporting military equipment to northern Russia. In 1922, on board the *Quest*, Shackleton died at South Georgia on his way yet again to fight the ice and danger. His wife decided that his body should be buried there within sound of the Antarctic seas, beneath a cairn built by his comrades on the *Quest*.

His explorations led to important scientific discoveries. He wrote about them in two books, *The Heart of the Antarctic* (1909), and *South* (1919).

(1856-1950)

George Bernard Shaw was born at 3 (now 33) Upper Synge Street, Dublin, on 26 July 1856. His mother was a fine singer and Shaw, from an early age, loved music. He began reading while very young and spent hours studying works of art in Dublin's National Gallery. He left school at the age of fifteen, working for a while as a clerk in an estate agent's office in Molesworth Street.

Moving to London in 1876, Shaw tried to earn a living by writing novels. Although his early literary career was unsuccessful, he never despaired and turned to reviewing, writing lively musical criticism under the name Corno di Bassetto. He also wrote art, drama and literary reviews for many magazines and newspapers.

Shaw was a great admirer of Ibsen and campaigned for plays dealing with current social and moral interests. He joined the Fabian Society which worked for improved social conditions, and read the works of Karl Marx whose socialist theories had a great influence on him. Initially a poor public speaker, he taught himself to be a marvellous debater and witty conversationalist, lecturing all over Britain.

A vegetarian, non-drinker and non-smoker, Shaw supported women's rights, equality of earnings, abolition of private property, changes in the voting system, new ways of spelling and a different alphabet. He was also a local government councillor for a while. Shaw was never idle, writing reviews, pamphlets or letters even as he travelled on trains and buses! This amazing energy remained with him even in old age: he bought his first motor bike when he was almost sixty and crashed it.

His first play, *Widowers' Houses*, about landlordism in London's slums, had only one performance when it was produced in 1892. Altogether Shaw wrote over fifty plays, including *Arms and the Man*, *Man and Superman*, *Major Barbara*, *Pygmalion* and *St Joan*. The hugely successful musical *My Fair Lady* was later based on *Pygmalion*. In 1898 he married Charlotte Payne Townshend who had nursed him through an illness during which he wrote *Caesar and Cleopatra*.

Shaw's plays were often debates in which the actors presented arguments for different beliefs and theories. His early experience as a public speaker helped his dramatic work. However, his popularity suffered when in 1914 he spoke out against Britain's participation in World War I. Shaw also opposed the execution of the Irish rebel, Roger Casement. His play, *The Shewing Up of Blanco Posnet*, was banned by the British Lord Chamberlain who considered it blasphemous, but it was later produced by Lady Gregory in Dublin's Abbey Theatre.

Shaw received the Nobel Prize for Literature in 1925 and was given the freedom of Dublin in 1946 at the age of 90. After a career as a dramatist spanning almost sixty years he died on 2 November 1950 at the age of 94 after an accident while gardening at his home. When he died, the lights were extinguished on Broadway, the heartland of American theatre, in his honour.

(1751-1816)

Richard Brinsley Sheridan was born at 12 Upper Dorset Street, Dublin, on 30 October 1751. He attended school at Samuel Whyte's Academy, Grafton Street (the site is now Bewley's Restaurant). It is hardly surprising that he was to achieve lasting fame as a playwright. His father was an actor and manager of Smock Alley Theatre, while his mother wrote novels and plays. Following the burning of Smock Alley after a riot in 1758, the family moved to London. After a few unhappy years at Harrow where Richard was a clever but lazy pupil, the Sheridans moved to Bath in 1770. There Richard's poetry began to appear in local journals.

In 1772 he ran away with Eliza Linley, a singer, to France. They were married near Calais, but the ceremony was invalid. To add to the difficulty Eliza was troubled by the attentions of another man with whom Sheridan fought two duels, wounding himself in the second. When the young couple returned to England, Richard's father tried to separate them, but they were legally married in 1773.

Sheridan became manager of Drury Lane Theatre. Perhaps influenced by his duelling experience his first play, *The Rivals*, was first performed at Covent Garden in 1775. The opening performance was unsuccessful, but wasting no time Sheridan rewrote the play. The new version, staged eleven nights later, received an enthusiastic reception. *The Rivals* is a comedy of manners showing Sheridan's skill in making fun of the way people behave. Among the many well-loved characters in the play is Mrs Malaprop whose habit of mixing up words is called Malapropism after her. In 1777 Sheridan's success earned him membership of Samuel Johnson's Literary Club. He had bought a half share of Drury Lane Theatre for £35,000, a huge sum at that time, buying the remainder in 1778 for a further £45,000.

Over the next few years, Sheridan wrote some of the most sparkling comedies in the English language including *The School for Scandal* (1777), his comic masterpiece, which exposes people in high society who delight in hurtful gossip, and *The Critic* (1779), a short satirical play attacking theatrical fashions.

Although he was considered by many to be the finest playwright since Shakespeare, his attention turned to politics. In 1780 he was elected Member of Parliament for Stafford. While serving in parliament he became friendly with Edmund Burke. However, unlike Burke, he supported the French Revolution and in a famous speech which lasted six hours, Sheridan passionately spoke out against the proposed union of Great Britain and Ireland.

Drury Lane Theatre, meanwhile, was going through a difficult period. Although Sheridan helped to launch the career of other younger playwrights, he himself wrote only one more work, *Pizarro* (1799). In 1809 the theatre was destroyed by fire leaving him penniless, and to add to his troubles, he lost his seat in the election of 1812.

His wife Eliza died in 1792 and three years later he married Esther Ogle. She was much younger than he. His last years were overshadowed by unhappiness. He was troubled by financial hardship (he was even imprisoned for debt) and by drunken quarrels with old friends.

Sheridan died on 7 July 1816. After a magnificent funeral through London he was buried in the Poets' Corner at Westminster Abbey.

A theatre fire ruined Richard Brinsley Sheridan

R. B. SHERIDAN

(1847-1912)

Abraham Stoker was born at 15 Marino Crescent, Fairview, on 8 November 1847, the son of a clerk at Dublin Castle. He was a quiet child and from an early age was a keen reader. During his student days in Trinity he developed an interest in theatre and was a fine athlete.

Although he joined the Civil Service in Dublin Castle, his love of the theatre turned his attention to journalism and he wrote drama reviews for the *Evening Mail*. A devoted fan of Sir Henry Irving, Stoker accepted the invitation to become Irving's secretary and manager of the Lyceum Theatre, London, in 1878, holding this position until Irving's death in 1905. The relationship was a demanding one, with Stoker often put under great pressure from his taxing master.

In 1878 Stoker married one-time friend of Oscar Wilde, Florence Balcombe. Despite his hectic workload, Stoker also managed to develop his own talents, and in 1897 his most famous novel, *Dracula*, was published. The book, a classic of gothic horror, was in part inspired by fellow Irishman, Sheridan Le Fanu's novel, *Carmilla* (1872), which dealt with vampirism. The character of Count Dracula himself has echoes of Stoker's hard master, Irving.

Although some of Stoker's other works, in particular, *The Lair of the White Worm* (1911), display a fine command of atmospheric horror, *Dracula* was the work with which Stoker will be forever associated. Following Irving's death, Stoker's *Personal Reminiscences of Henry Irving* was published in 1906.

Bram Stoker died in 1912, survived by his wife and son. Since then his masterpiece, *Dracula*, has been filmed many times. Translations of the work have ensured that the character of the sinister Count from Transylvania has continued to capture the world's imagination.

(1667-1745)

Jonathan Swift was born near Werburgh Street, Dublin, on 30 November 1667. Although his father died before Jonathan's birth, he was educated well through the aid of a relative, and at fourteen was one of the youngest entrants to Trinity College, having attended Kilkenny Grammar School. Accused of indiscipline at Trinity, he was nearly refused his degree.

In 1689 he travelled to England and became private secretary to Sir William Temple of Moor Park, an old friend of the Swift family. Temple treated him like a son advising him on his writing style. It was here that Swift wrote his early poetry and also became tutor to Esther Johnson, the beloved Stella of his writings. Their friendship lasted until her death in 1727.

He decided to join the Church, leaving England against Temple's wishes. Expecting a good position, Swift found himself as a country vicar to three poor parishes in Antrim. However, he made important literary and political friends. The English government, recognising his talent, engaged him to write pamphlets. Returning to London Swift became famous as a wit and political writer. In 1704 *A Tale of a Tub* was published, ridiculing divisions in religion and learning. Swift's other satirical work, *The Battle of the Books*, was popular but annoyed important people in Church and parliament.

His *Journal to Stella* (1710–13), written for his young friend, describes London life, its world of politics and power. Swift loved good company, food, cards, swimming, horseriding and walking. Around this time he met Esther Vanhomrigh, the woman of his poem, 'Cadenus and Vanessa' (1713).

After a long wait for promotion, he became Dean of St Patrick's Cathedral in Dublin. He often criticised the British government's neglect of Ireland. His 'Proposal for the Universal Use of Irish Manufactures' (1720) advised people to buy Irish goods, and to burn everything British but their coal.

The Drapier Letters (1724) condemned the introduction of inferior Irish coinage as British exploitation. Swift also criticised the Irish for laziness and dishonesty. In *A Modest Proposal* (1729) Swift mockingly suggested that Ireland's poor children should be sold to feed the wealthy.

He worked hard in his church, preaching, visiting the sick and organising a choir.

His major work, *Gulliver's Travels* (1726), is a classic children's story. However, it also exposes the pride and corruption of humanity and so appeals to all ages.

Swift's last years were unhappy. In 1742 he suffered a stroke which left him speechless. He died on 19 October 1745 and was buried beside Stella in the grounds of St Patrick's Cathedral. Leaving his money to build a hospital for the insane, he humorously observed that no country needed it so much.

Swift and Stella

(1871-1909)

John Millington Synge was born in Rath-farnham, Dublin, on 16 April 1871, the youngest of a family of eight. His father, a barrister and landowner of the Protestant Anglo-Irish class, died when John was an infant. Suffering from poor eyesight, he received much of his early education at home. In 1892 he graduated from Trinity College winning a prize in Irish. A capable violinist, he left to study music in France and Germany, but abandoned his musical career in 1894 to teach English in Paris. There he met William Butler Yeats who advised him to visit the Aran Islands in Galway Bay and to explore the native culture. His travels there were to be the turning point of his life. Synge was fascinated by the primitive simplicity of the islanders' lives and the richness of their speech. Synge's early interest in nature also developed in his travels through Mayo, Kerry and Wicklow, but it was the stories and folklore of Aran which inspired his future work.

In 1904 he became Director of the Abbey Theatre. With Yeats and Lady Gregory he was a leading figure in the Irish Literary Revival. Synge now embarked on his brief but productive period as a dramatist. His plays, drawing on his early experiences in Connemara and Aran, were written in a style which brought the power and richness of Irish to the English language.

His one-act play, *The Shadow of the Glen* (1903), was criticised because it presented a loveless Irish marriage. His powerful tragedy, *Riders to the Sea* (1904), produced in London, was based on a drowning disaster in Aran, where a mother lost all four of her sons. *The Well of the Saints* was staged at the Abbey in 1905. Synge was also kept busy with a series for an English newspaper, the *Manchester Guardian*, about social conditions in the west of Ireland.

He fell in love with an Abbey actress, Molly Allgood, whose stage name was Máire O'Neill. For her Synge wrote many fine poems and the part of Pegeen Mike in his masterpiece, *The Playboy of the Western World* (1907), considered by many to be one of the greatest plays to come out of Ireland. This play, exposing bigotry, hypocrisy and cruelty, sparked off riots in the Abbey when Synge suggested that Irish peasants would condone a murder and harbour the killer. Policemen were called in to remove fighting protesters. The play toured England later with great success, but it again caused riots when staged in American cities in 1910, where the actors were arrested on one occasion.

From 1897 Synge suffered from Hodgkin's disease. His final play, *Deirdre of the Sorrows*, was only half completed when he died on 24 March 1909. *Deirdre* and *The Tinker's Wedding* were staged after his death. In his short life John Millington Synge wrote plays of great power and beauty. He is buried in Mount Jerome Cemetery, Dublin.

*The **Playboy** caused a riot in the Abbey Theatre*

JOHN MILLINGTON SYNGE

(1763-1798)

Theobald Wolfe Tone was born probably in Stafford Street (now called Wolfe Tone Street), Dublin, on 20 June 1763. His father, who was a coachmaker, returned to the family farm in Bodenstown, Co. Kildare, and settled there in 1778.

Theobald was sent to Trinity College in 1781. However, he had never liked school and did not enjoy his work at Trinity. But he did participate in the lively college atmosphere and won medals for speaking at the Historical Society's debates. He also enjoyed the social life of Dublin.

In 1785 he eloped with a fifteen-year-old girl, Matilda Witterington. After a while Tone completed his studies, obtaining a BA in 1786. Eventually he went to London to study for a legal career. He tried to join the British Army at one stage, hoping for service in India, but his application was too late. In 1788 he returned to Dublin, bought £100 worth of law books and took his law degree in Trinity the following year hoping to earn his living as a lawyer.

Gradually he became involved in the movements for Irish independence, writing pamphlets and articles in support of his views. The British government, through spies and informers, began to keep a watchful eye on Tone. In October 1791 the Society of United Irishmen was founded in Belfast. Soon afterwards Tone and his friend, Thomas Russell, established a branch in Dublin. Members included Rowan Hamilton and Napper Tandy. Many of them were inspired by the French Revolution and its cry for equality. They hoped to win full civil rights for Catholics.

In 1791, the Protestant Tone was appointed Secretary to the Catholic Committee, a body formed to press for the repeal of the remaining penal laws. The following year, he accompanied a Catholic Committee delegation to London to present a petition to the king. Although the British government partly conceded by passing a Relief Act in 1793, which gave Catholics voting rights, a Catholic could not become a judge or enter parliament.

France and England were then at war. The United Irishmen hoped for French assistance in their struggle for independence. French agent William Jackson visited Dublin in 1794, but the British were following him and Tone found himself in danger. Almost arrested, he sailed to America in 1795.

Before long he departed for France, arriving there in 1796 under the name James Smith. He hoped to organise a French invasion of Ireland to drive out the British. The French listened carefully, seeing this as an opportunity to attack England by controlling Irish ports. Tone's request was granted.

On 2 December 1796 he sailed in a fleet of forty-three ships carrying almost 15,000 men bound for Ireland. But rocked by storms, the ships were scattered, and after waiting in terrible weather at Bantry Bay, Tone returned to France.

As Tone waited impatiently for the French to organise another fleet, many of his United Irishmen comrades had been arrested. At last in September 1798 a French fleet sailed from Brest to join an earlier invasion force under Humbert. It was led by Hardy and aboard the flagship, *Hoche*, was Wolfe Tone.

Unfortunately the *Hoche* was forced to surrender after a four-hour naval battle in Lough Swilly against a superior English force. Tone was arrested and placed on trial for treason in Dublin. Wearing a French uniform he asked to be shot like a soldier. This wish was refused and Tone was condemned to death by hanging. Although mystery surrounds his death, most sources claim that he cut his own throat in jail on 11 November 1798 and died on the 19th. His journals were published in America by his son, William, in 1826.

Battle of Vinegar Hill, 1798

THEOBALD WOLFE TONE

(1769-1852)

Arthur Wellesley, known as the Iron Duke, became famous as the general who defeated Napoleon at the Battle of Waterloo. He was also leader of the Tory Party and served as Prime Minister of Great Britain.

Arthur Wellesley was born at Mornington House, 24 Upper Merrion Street, Dublin, on 1 May 1769. His father, the Earl of Mornington, died when Arthur was twelve. Three years later his mother sent him to a military college at Angers where he learned French and horseriding. Eventually he entered the army in 1787, serving a tough winter campaign in Flanders (1794–95). Largely because of his eldest brother's political influence, Wellesley was soon promoted and by 1796 was made Colonel, fighting with his regiment in India. Meanwhile he had also entered the political battlefield representing Trim in parliament from 1790 to 1795. He spoke out aggressively against France and, although supporting the granting of votes to Catholics, disapproved of their admission to parliament.

Wellesley was a shrewd leader and military planner, calculating the amount of food an army needed, the weight it could carry and the distance it could travel. In 1801 he was sent to Egypt to face the man who was to become his greatest enemy, Napoleon Bonaparte. Bonaparte was at this time building up an empire for France. However, Wellesley was laid low by fever. It was a lucky illness because the ship in which he was to have sailed sank in the Red Sea without survivors.

In 1803 he was made Commander of the British forces during a series of battles in India. Although outnumbered, he attacked the enemy at Assaye and, despite heavy loss of life, won the battle.

He was knighted for his exceptional military service in 1804, became a Member of Parliament for Rhye in 1806 and later Secretary for Ireland (1807–9). During his office in Ireland he worked to reduce rents and to establish a police force.

Meanwhile, Napoleon's power was spreading throughout Europe. In 1808 the Peninsular War began (so called because the battles were fought in the peninsula of Spain and Portugal). The Spaniards revolted when Napoleon made his brother King of Spain and they asked England for help. Wellesley was promoted to Lieutenant-General and sailed with 10,000 men to Spain. He defeated the French at the Battle of Vimeiro in Portugal. In 1809 Wellesley became overall Commander of the British forces in Europe. Although he received little help from the inefficient armies of Spain and Portugal, his smaller force won battle after battle, slowly driving the French from the peninsula and moving steadily northwards towards France.

In April 1814, Wellesley, newly created a Viscount, won the Battle of Toulouse, enabling British troops to enter France. Following Napoleon's surrender, the war came to an end. Wellesley returned in triumph to England and was given the title by which he is best known, the Duke of Wellington.

In July 1814 Wellington was appointed Ambassador to France, representing Great Britain the following year at the great Congress of Vienna. The amazed congress heard of Napoleon's escape from imprisonment on the island of Elba, his return to France and his preparations to make himself master of Europe again. Wellington led his army once more into the heat of battle, finally facing his old rival on 18 June 1815 at the village of Waterloo in Belgium. In this battle Wellington completely crushed Napoleon's army. Napoleon was exiled to St Helena where he died six years later.

In 1819 Wellington became a member of the Cabinet and by 1828 was Prime Minister. Wellington, who belonged to the Tory Party, upset many of his colleagues by pushing through an Act of Parliament which granted the vote to Roman Catholics. The Tories were defeated in 1830, and although they were returned to power in 1834, Wellington refused to become Prime Minister again. He retired from public office in 1846.

Although the old soldier's blunt speaking and his tough position on political reform made him unpopular at times, he was respected as a national hero. On his death in 1852 he was buried, after a huge funeral, in St Paul's Cathedral, beside the body of Admiral Nelson.

Wellington at Waterloo

(1916-   )

Thomas Kenneth Whitaker, architect of the modern Irish economy, was born in Rostrevor, Co. Down, on 8 December 1916. After moving to Drogheda in 1922 he was educated at the local Christian Brothers School. In 1934 he entered the Civil Service, and was attached to the Department of Finance from 1938 to 1969. In 1941 he was married to Nora Fogarty; they have six children. He received a Masters in Sciences (Econ.) at London University by private study.

His exceptional abilities resulted in him being appointed Secretary of the Department of Finance, holding the position from May 1956 to February 1969. In the following month he became Governor of the Central Bank (March 1969 to February 1976), having been a director since 1958.

Playing a major role in developing the conditions necessary for economic expansion during the late 1950s and 1960s, he was mainly responsible for the study, 'Economic Development', of August 1958, a watershed in Ireland's economic history. This document highlighted the shortcomings and possibilities of the economy, suggesting strategies for future growth such as the necessity of productive investment, flexible planning, improved management, and education. Perhaps its overwhelming achievement was in dissipating a prevailing economic pessimism. Recognised as a valuable constructive approach to the formulation of economic policies suitable to Irish conditions, it was the basis for the government's White Paper published in November 1958, the First Programme for Economic Expansion.

He accompanied the then Taoiseach, Sean Lemass, on his historic visit to the Stormont Northern Ireland Parliament in 1965 and helped arrange the meeting between Lemass and the Northern Premier, Terence O'Neill. His many public involvements chart an amazing record of his wide range of interests serving as president, chairman and director on numerous boards, institutions and councils.

Besides his 'Economic Development', his outstanding policy report of 1958 which laid the basis for the boom of the 1960s, he is the author of *Financing by Credit Creation* (1946), *Interests* (1983), papers to the Statistical and Social Inquiry Society of Ireland, as well as several articles in *Studies* and many other periodicals spanning forty years.

Recognitions include an Honorary Doctorate of Economic Science (National University of Ireland 1962), LL.D. (University of Dublin 1976), LL.D. (Queen's University, Belfast 1980), D.Sc. (University of Ulster 1984) and Commandeur de la Legion d'Honneur (1976). In 1991 he became a member of the Council of State, chosen by President Robinson. In the same year, he chaired the Common Fisheries Policy Review.

(1854–1900)

Oscar Fingal O'Flahertie Wills Wilde was born at 21 Westland Row on 16 October 1854. His father was an eminent eye and ear specialist; his mother was a poetess and folklorist. Educated at Portora Royal School, Enniskillen, he won a scholarship in 1871 to Trinity College, Dublin. Three years later he left Ireland to study at Oxford University where he distinguished himself as a scholar and wit. Oscar's eccentricity of dress also attracted attention. He was a popular figure in high society even before his literary talent was recognised. Here he won the Newdigate prize for poetry in 1879. In 1882, he toured the United States and Canada lecturing on philosophy. On his return, he married Constance Lloyd in 1884.

Wilde published a volume of poems, largely romantic in style, in 1881. But it was the publication of *The Happy Prince and Other Tales* (1888) which marked the start of his literary career. His only novel, *The Picture of Dorian Gray* (1890), is a moral fable. The strange story is about a man whose portrait ages and grows ugly as a reflection of his moral decay, while his own physical appearance remains unchanged.

The plays of Oscar Wilde, however, are his most significant achievements. *Lady Windermere's Fan* (1892), *A Woman of No Importance* (1893) and *An Ideal Husband* (1895) combine the drama of social intrigue with marvellous comic dialogue which echoes Wilde's own dazzling conversational powers. In *The Importance of Being Earnest* (1895) Wilde, as he did in much of his work, ridiculed social hypocrisy and the ideals of earnestness and sincerity.

He wrote *Salome* in French (1893), a one-act biblical tragedy which was translated by Lord Alfred Douglas who was Oscar's constant companion. In 1895 Wilde's career was at its zenith with three hit plays running at the same time to packed audiences. However, in the same year he was accused of having a homosexual relationship with Lord Alfred Douglas by Douglas's father. At that time in England, homosexual practice was a criminal offence. Wilde became involved in a famous court battle as a result of which he was sentenced to two years' hard labour in May 1895. Wilde's most powerful poem, 'The Ballad of Reading Gaol' (1898), is hewn from his prison experience, a punishment doubly difficult for a sensitive man who had enjoyed the soft life of luxury and high society up to then. He also wrote an autobiographical essay, *De Profundis*, developed from a long letter to Lord Alfred Douglas, which was influenced by his term in prison.

On his release Wilde left England, spending the rest of his life in Italy and France, dependent on the financial generosity of friends. Broken in health, drained of creative energy and in financial trouble he died of cerebral meningitis at the Hotel D'Alsace, Paris, on 30 November 1900, after receiving the last rites of the Catholic Church. He is buried at Père Lachaise Cemetery in Paris.

(1938-)

Michael Terence Wogan was born on 3 August 1938 in Limerick. His father was the managing director of a grocery and wine chain. Educated at Limerick's Crescent College, he later attended Belvedere College when the family moved to Dublin in 1953.

Although Terry worked as a bank clerk for five years he was destined for a career other than in finance. Having answered a newspaper advertisement for the position of announcer/newsreader in Radio Éireann, he began his broadcasting life in 1961 with a cattle market report and a popular light music programme, 'Hospital's Requests'. He also worked on the fledgling television station RTE as an announcer.

He married former model, Helen Joyce, and the couple had three children. In 1967 he approached the BBC and, after standing in for his idol, veteran broadcaster, Jimmy Young, he established himself as a regular on BBC radio. For the first two years he commuted between England and Ireland before committing himself to the wider British market.

Down through the years his easy-going manner, light-hearted banter and infectious humour have endeared him to millions of listeners and viewers. His growing popularity with radio listeners made him a household name when he presented BBC Radio 2's breakfast programme. Radio shows such as 'The Terry Wogan Show'; 'Pop Score'; 'Punchline'; 'Twenty Questions'; 'Quote, Unquote'; 'Year in Question' and television programmes like 'Lunchtime with Wogan'; 'Come Dancing'; 'Miss World'; 'Eurovision Song Contest'; 'Song for Europe'; 'Blankety Blank'; 'Variety Club Awards'; 'Disco'; 'Startown'; 'What's on Wogan?'; 'You Must Be Joking', and 'Wogan' have made him a national institution throughout Great Britain and Ireland.

Among the many awards acknowledging his contribution to radio and television are Radio Personality of the Year, TV Times Award for Most Popular TV Personality (seven years in a row), Variety Club Award (Radio Personality) and the Pye Radio Award.

The format of his current programme, 'Wogan', broadcast three times a week, suits his light, cheerful style. Its mixture of affable conversation interspersed with musical acts has proved such a popular combination that the silver-tongued Irishman has been contracted until 1992 for a fee worth £1 million. He was closely involved in the establishment of Century Radio in his native Ireland until its closure in 1991.

A brief flirtation with the world of popular music resulted in his song, 'The Floral Dance' enjoying great success. In 1989 he wrote *Wogan's Ireland*. Probably the Irish face most frequently seen on British television, with its audience of almost 80 million people, he lives a quiet life with his wife Helen and family of three near Maidenhead in Berkshire. A keen golfer, he is well known for his work organising celebrity tournaments for various charities.

(1871-1957)

Jack Butler Yeats, the youngest of five children, was born in London on 29 August 1871. His father was the painter John B. Yeats. When the youngster was eight years of age he went to live with his mother's parents in Sligo which became for him, like his brother, William, a place of inspiration. There Jack sketched Sligo's streets and port, and painted landscapes of the surrounding countryside. In 1887 he returned to London to study art and was soon contributing illustrations of boxing and horse-racing to magazines such as *The Vegetarian* and *Paddock Life*.

In 1894 Yeats married Mary White, a Devon artist. Three years later they left London to settle in Devon. In 1895 his water-colour, 'Strand Races, West of Ireland', was accepted by the Royal Hibernian Academy. With the development of photography at this time, traditional illustrations were less in demand. Realising this Yeats decided to concentrate on painting, with scenes from his Sligo childhood, circus performers, meetings and itinerants. He held exhibitions in London and Dublin, being the first Irish artist to hold one-man shows at the Tate and the National Galleries in London.

Jack and his wife kept up contact with Ireland, visiting Lady Gregory at Coole, and visiting his beloved Sligo every summer. He and Synge joined forces for a walking tour in the west of Ireland. Yeats later illustrated articles by Synge on congested districts in the west and also his book, *The Aran Islands*. In 1912 Jack published *Life in the West of Ireland*, a book of paintings and drawings. His popularity was now spreading and he held one-man exhibitions in New York in 1913. In 1910 they had moved from Devon to Greystones, Co. Wicklow, and from there to Dublin seven years later. It was a turbulent period in Ireland with the Rebellion in 1916 leading to two wars within the following six years.

His paintings, mostly in oil, from this time reflected the disturbed times. The precise draughtsmanship of his earlier work was gradually replaced by the use of rich colour and broad brushwork. His reputation steadily grew with a successful retrospective exhibition at the National Gallery, London, in 1942. Further exhibitions followed in the

National College of Art, Dublin (1945), the Tate Gallery, London (1948), and a touring exhibition throughout America in 1951.

Many of his paintings are stories set out on canvas, so it was not totally out of character for him to try his hand at writing. Memoirs such as *Sligo* (1930), *Ah Well* (1942), *And to You Also* (1944); novels including *Sailing, Sailing Swiftly* (1933) and *The Aramanthers* (1936); and plays such as *La La Noo* (1942) and *In Sand* (1949) display his versatility, but lacked the creative impact of his paintings. He received many honours including honorary degrees from several universities and the Legion of Honour. He died in Dublin on 28 March 1957 and was buried in Mount Jerome Cemetery. Since his death his reputation has soared, his work now realising huge sums of money.

Yeats's painting 'The Liffey Swim'

(1865-1939)

William Butler Yeats, perhaps the greatest modern poet in the English language, was born at 5 Sandymount Avenue, Dublin, on 13 June 1865. The family moved to London but Yeats spent long childhood holidays in Sligo with his grandparents. Returning to Dublin in 1800, he studied art and became interested in mysticism.

Since boyhood he had loved Irish legends and folklore and through these became involved in Irish nationalism. He investigated the world of magic as a member of the Theosophical Society and the Order of the Golden Dawn. His early volume of poetry, *The Wanderings of Oisín and Other Poems*, reflects his fascination with mythology. In

1891 Yeats founded the Irish Literary Society whose members included leading Irish writers.

He fell in love with Maud Gonne, an actress revolutionary. She rejected his marriage proposal but figured prominently in Yeats's poetry and acted in his play, *The Countess Cathleen*. The play was staged by the Irish Literary Theatre founded by himself and his lifelong friend Lady Gregory. Impressed by Maud Gonne's revolutionary activities, Yeats for a while became interested in the Republican movement.

His play, *On Baile's Strand* (1904), was performed at the opening of the Abbey Theatre (where he remained a director throughout his life). Other plays included *The Land of Hearts Desire* and *The Words upon the Window Pain*. Yeats's drama was totally different to the realistic plays popular at the time. The dream-like movement, symbol, myth and poetic language of his work was influenced by Japanese Noh theatre, where mask, mime and chanting were important features. Yeats dominated every phase of the Abbey Theatre's development from its origin until his death.

However, Yeats was, above all, famous as a poet with several volumes to his credit. An American lecture tour (1903–4) established his name in that country.

The sacrifice of the Easter Rising surprised Yeats and moved him to write in 'Easter 1916':

> All changed, changed utterly
> A terrible beauty is born.

The savagery of war led him to worry whether his revolutionary play, *The Countess Cathleen* had led men to their deaths.

> Did that play of mine send out
> Certain men the English shot?

In 1917 Yeats married George Hyde-Lees, an English spiritualist who influenced some of his poetry. He bought a summer house at Thoor Ballylee, a restored Norman tower in Co. Galway which became a special place for him, a poetic symbol. His wife being a medium, he encouraged her to record the supernatural messages she received. In 'A Vision' (1925) he set out his ideas on mankind and art using some of his wife's material.

Unlike many major poets, Yeats's greatest work was written during his old age. Some of his most passionate poems, bristling with energy, were composed in the last twenty years of his life, volumes such as *The Tower* (1928) and *Winding Stairs and other Poems* (1933). He became a Senator, and among other honours received the Nobel Prize for Literature in 1923. He and George Bernard Shaw founded the Irish Academy of Letters in 1932.

For health reasons Yeats spent his last winters in France. He died at Rocquebrune in the north of France on 28 January 1939. His remains were brought home to Ireland in 1948 and reinterred at Drumcliffe, Co. Sligo. His words, chiselled on the tombstone are well known:

> Cast a cold eye
> On life, on death.
> Horseman, pass by!

*An Abbey Theatre production of Yeats's **Deirdre***

WILLIAM BUTLER YEATS